A WALK OF LOVE

An autobiography of Papa Joe Bradford

by
Papa Joe Bradford

A Walk of Love
by Papa Joe Bradford

Printed in the United States of America

ISBN 9781622304332

www.xulonpress.com

Dedication

I dedicate this book to the children all over the world in need of rescue from the emotional and physical pains that come from poverty and oppression of various forms.

I dedicate this book to all who are praying and striving diligently to make a positive change in the lives of those who are less fortunate.

I especially dedicate this book to those destined to grow in a deeper walk of love. I pray that this book will be an inspiration to transform hearts into a fire of passion that results in greater "love in action" toward others.

Contents

ACKNOWLEDGMENTS

M any friends and family supported and prayed for me in the writing of this book in which I am humbly thankful, but I choose to mention a few by name.

I graciously thank Terry Poore for pouring years of expertise into the manuscript and abolishing my typographical sins.

My heart felt thanks to Kelly Lentz, who helped tremendously by providing support and hours of discussion.

I am deeply grateful to Tom and Tami Golden, who dedicated precious time to give invaluable suggestions, which came from years of ministry experience.

I sincerely thank Dr. Jennifer Coleman, who had a profound effect on this writing through her spirit of excellence.

I am especially grateful for Nicky Brandon, whose walk of love with my family within the inner city is a memoir that helped fuel my inspiration to write.

My special thanks goes to Julia and Andrew Ingle, who shared their immense creativity and counsel in writing the book and designing the covers.

My deep appreciation goes to Theresa Lyles and (the belated Elvis D. Lyles), who gave birth to and raised my godly queen, Denise. Thanks for your love.

My forever thanks goes to my mother Nancy Bradford, sister Sonya Daniels, (and belated grandmother Elizabeth Mays), whose prayers covered decades of my life. Thanks for your love.

My treasured thanks goes to my children (Chazn, Caylin, Jordan, Elijah, Johnathan, Shadai, and Kyla), who are a blessed sign of our ministry to children throughout the world.

My most treasured thanks goes to my wife, Denise, who is my collaborative writer and has been my greatest encourager and closest friend. You inspired me to make no secret of my past struggles and sins in order to point to the awesome transformation that comes through God's grace.

My highest honor, thanks, praise and glory forever goes to my King Jesus; Who is my inspiration and life. Thank You for introducing me to my eternal Father.

Introduction

I love listening to the sound of angels, joyfully singing beautiful, melodious songs. The purity of the sound is so serene and captivating, one could be sure that the tangible touch of God's very hand sweeps over the entire atmosphere with His own breath. I can feel the sound and I can even see the sound appearing as fantastic colors of light. *Is this what sound looks like? Could this be real? I am in pure bliss in this moment. This must be the sound of heaven.* That's what I hear and feel while the inner city children sing the songs I just taught them. How could this sound come from little ones who have so little and experience so much? Their world is filled with the sound of sirens, gunshots, violence, cursing, and negative criticisms. These are the typical sounds they hear, yet they produce something so lovely and wonderful. This is a mystery.

Oh, how I empathize with the lives of the children so full of tragedy, needing someone to notice their silent cries. As I watch them sing together, it's exhilarating as the chaos in their minds is transformed into joy. God's music truly is a universal language. Can you imagine the anticipation of the children each week before my wife Denise and I gather them for choir? They look at me with inquisitive eyes, because I am a rare commodity in their neighborhood; a man free from drugs and alcohol, married to a woman he loves, rearing his own children, and most of all taking time out for them.

Abused Child

One Saturday afternoon, it was time to wrap up and close the rehearsal. Something caught my attention: a child who had been beaten. It was a girl around twelve years old. Dark painful bruises covered her swollen face. *How could anyone do this?* For a moment, feelings of great despair for this child troubled me. It was important for the morale of this abused child that I quickly regain my composure. She walked over to me, allowing me to see her pain, and uncontrollable tears started to roll down her cheeks. On the outside, I hugged and comforted her. On the inside, I fought hard to resist the urge to seek and destroy the culprit. The old warrior inside me craved physical justice. I've been a fighter all my life. Only through the grace of God could I withstand against the residue in my heart of past battles.

I took several of our choir leaders to her home to investigate the incident while other leaders stayed with the choir. When we got to the child's home, we were faced with an unexpected situation. A family member informed us that the child's drug induced mother had beaten her in a fit of rage. It was shocking that the perpetrator was not an abusive boy friend or father figure, which was normally the case in a situation like this. Unfortunately, the family did not even know the identity of the child's father. The necessary precautions were taken to prevent a recurrence of the situation. I could hear my mind wondering, *now what? Is my job done here?*

Life-Defining Moment

When we arrived back at the choir rehearsal, I was in desperate need to sit alone for a moment. So I sat with my mind racing over all that I had just experienced and witnessed with my own eyes. It exhausted me as I felt my strength leave me. The other children of the choir were enjoying a snack not too many feet from where I sat. The abused child's seven-year-old sister noticed me and came over as if she needed to ask me a question. My heart started to pound rapidly as I anticipated her concern: *Oh no, why was she coming over to me? Was she going to ask me what happened with their mother? Was she afraid that she too would be next in line for a beating?* I prepared myself to answer her questions about her mother. Then the little girl looked me in the eyes and simply asked a question I will never forget: "Will you be my daddy?"

I was speechless...she did not flinch as she awaited my answer. Obviously, she didn't know that I too had been a fatherless child. She didn't know my dad abandoned me when I was in my mother's womb. She was unaware of an affectionate father's ways. Interestingly, she didn't request an interview to determine my qualifications. She didn't require a background check on my past. She didn't even concern herself if I had succeeded in being a father before. Innocently, she simply stared at the love in my heart that I didn't even know I had, and she looked at me with those big brown eyes and asked again, "Will you be my daddy?"

Although I've attempted, words cannot fully express what I felt in that life-changing moment. My heart was arrested with love that flowed from the depths of my soul and throughout my being as this question was asked by such a sweet, desperate, helpless, hopeless, fatherless child.

I turned to my right because I heard footsteps of another little girl approaching quickly. For a moment, I thought this bought me some time to stall on the question, but without my knowledge this second child had heard the first girl's inquiry. She was rushing to me because she too wanted to submit her request. Sounding as though she had a fear of being left out, she too asked, "Will you be my daddy?" I stood there and wondered: *"Was this a game they were playing with me? Had they planned this? Were they serious?"*

At that moment I believe God did something to answer my speculations. Suddenly a little boy who also had been watching came to my left and quickly asked: "Will you be my daddy?" Another little boy was just behind him and echoed, "Will you be my daddy?" Then another child whose face I did not see inquired from behind me: "Will you be my daddy?" The sound of many footsteps was coming my way. I found myself in total disarray as this choir of desperate fatherless children converged upon me and surrounded me without shame, hoping, needing, and begging for the answer to one question: "Will you be my daddy?"

They didn't plan this scenario. There was no game in their hearts. It was as if time stood still as this small crowd of children stared in anticipation to this one important question: "Will you be my daddy?" It was as if the Holy Spirit took hot oil and poured it over my heart melting any areas reluctant to give all I could be to these children. In other words, my love increased even more for them. The Lord had humbled me to experience an indescribable passion of love for each child surrounding me.

I did not answer their question directly. I just smiled at them and said, "I love all of you." When I returned home from choir rehearsal and sat alone with God, the answer to all the children that day became inevitably clear as I heard a voice in my heart saying: "From now on you shall be called, 'Papa Joe.'"

The Awakening

It was then I realized that the tragedy, violence, heartache, torture, suffering, and so much loss in my life turned out to be the vital experience that propelled me into my destiny. Through all my pain and sacrifice, hope was always within reach and transformation was just around the corner. Little did I know that the very experiences that caused me to be an advocate for oppressed children would inspire producers of a major motion picture to choose my life to encourage and motivate others such as you to travel this walk of love to rescue others in dire need.

I am convinced that this journey will challenge you to believe that you can make a difference in the lives of those less fortunate throughout the world. I will be as open and transparent as humanly possible as to how "Papa Joe" fully came to be, how an amazing union with Denise resulted in overcoming many seemingly insurmountable obstacles, and how tragedy can turn into triumph.

Denise and I are inviting you to join us on this walk of love. As we take this stroll together, I pray you too will encounter that same love I felt on the day I was asked the big question, "Will you be my daddy?" In all my living days, I never would have thought "I" could be so needed and desired in such a significant and powerful way.

And now, journey with me into presenting the unusual, challenging and death-defying experiences that formed my walk of love from the very beginning...

Chapter 1

THE FIRST BLACK SAMURAI

It is the end of the year, 1964, during the festive Christmas holiday season. I am a three-year-old African American boy living with my grandmother, mother, and older sister in my grandmother's little four-room impoverished country home complete with an outhouse and new indoor running water (we filled in the well in our back yard with dirt.) That was so exciting! We are moving on up! Love and excitement bubbles in my heart. To top it all off, my dad is coming to take my mother, sister, and me to visit his family in the big city: Nashville. Up to that point, I'd only ever seen him twice. He left my mama when I was in her womb. Questions fill my mind. *What is he like? Is he strong enough to pick me up? Is he here to stay? Most of all does he love me like I love him?*

In America, this is one of the most ground-shaking years to begin uniting our country into greatness. President Lyndon B. Johnson declares a "War on Poverty" giving birth to food stamps. The famous Civil Rights Act is passed, making segregation of black and white folk in public facilities and racial discrimination in employment illegal. A black man named Martin Luther King Jr. wins the Nobel Peace Prize. Fear of the Ku Klux Klan tormenting unsuspecting Negro drivers on the back roads is ever present. The Vietnam War is escalating. Turbulence is at hand. I was too young to consider the dangers of the fast changing world around me. Though it's a season of magnified hatred and prejudice in the country and all around me, it does not change my heart. At this point, I simply have not yet learned how to hate.

All I seem to focus on and want is the love of my father whom I've rarely seen. I don't care why he left me. I don't care about the disagreements over money that he and my mother had over rearing a second child. I don't care why he hasn't come to see me. I don't care that he might have wanted a better son because I am so slow of speech. There are no conditions necessary for me to love him. I just do.

Toddler Logic

I obey Mama in love, because she knows best. I obey Grandmama, because- well I like to sit down without pain. If my big sister annoys me, or more likely I annoy her, we fight and then make up. If I'm the last to cross the finish line in the neighborhood race, I just throw dirt in the other kids' faces and then try to run away. But then they catch and destroy me as I forget that they can outrun me. I quickly forgive them, and back to the races we go. Life is easy. Love is easy…oh, the joys of being a kid. And boy oh boy, the joy of being me today, because my dad is coming to take my mom, sister, and me for a car ride to Nashville- the big, big city! I will never forget the day I saw my daddy.

Everybody says we look just alike and boy oh boy we do! I can't take my eyes off of him. His eyes are just like mine. And his lips are just like mine too! Will my voice sound like his when

I grow up? I wonder if we laugh alike; do we
like the same food? Do I look like him when
he was a boy? My eyes were just glued on my
daddy. And his voice is deep, but gentle. He is
really nice, but he doesn't talk much.

On the way back home is my big chance to
prove to Dad that I love him so much and that
I am worthy of his love. I was a good boy
when I met his mother, my other grandmother,
today. I even smiled when she hugged me
with that yucky brown juice rolling down her
chin. Snuff: it was nasty. My dad stops to get
gas. Once in the station, I couldn't help but to
notice that there is a toy for sale that I figured
every dad wants his son to have: the coveted
Johnny Eagle Special Edition Rifle.

Surely, this is it! I suddenly have this great idea
and try super hard to explain to my dad how
proud I will make him if he buys me that rifle. I
will blast all the bad guys in his life, especially
the ones he told mama that are keeping him
from getting a job close to our home. My dad
says the most glorious words that I have ever
heard in my life, "Let's buy the Johnny Eagle
Special Edition Rifle right now, and I will let
you kill all the bad guys that keep us apart."
With joy, I watch my dad reach for the toy rifle
when my mother abruptly exclaims, "No! If
you buy the toy now, it will spoil your son, and
he will expect me to buy him other toys for no
reason. Wait and bring it when you come to
see him in three weeks for Christmas."

My mother's words nearly crush my heart into tiny pieces; Mama is ruining my opportunity to prove myself to Daddy, yet there is a ray of hope. Not getting the toy rifle now means that he will be coming back for Christmas. Now, I'm overjoyed with expectation, but dad on the other hand is upset with Mama. They argue all the way home. When we arrive on the country dirt road where we live, my dad strangely parks the car a few feet before reaching our house. We cannot see our house from here, because of the neighbor's hedge bushes. Why is he parked here? Maybe he doesn't want Grandmama to know we are back to avoid fighting with her also.

My dad walks my mom, sister, and me to the door. Without so much as a smile he says, "bye." As he quickly walks away, I yell to him, "See you at Christmas." No answer. I watch him disappear behind the hedge bushes and hear his car drive away. In confusion, I head to my room with my heart heavy.

I'm not exactly sure when Christmas is, but I expect that I will see my daddy soon. Not a day passes until Christmas that I don't get on Mama's nerves asking, "When is daddy coming home?" Each time, she smiles just a little, but not a big smile like mine. The smile went away too fast. Why isn't mommy happy like me? Then at last, it is Christmas day! I awake early and look out the window all morning for hours, waiting to see dad show up from beside the hedge bushes. But through

my extreme discouragement and salty tears,
he does not appear.

After that Nashville trip when I watched my dad dash
pass the neighbor's hedge bushes, I would not touch, see,
nor hear his voice again—for over 20 years.

Childish Optimism
For the next several years during the holiday season I
would ask my mama, "Is daddy coming home?" Maybe he
meant a different Christmas. I would look out the window
early every Christmas morning hoping he would keep his
promise and bring me the Johnny Eagle Special Edition
Rifle to shoot all the enemies that keep us apart. I thought
that surely a dad would want his son around to play baseball,
race hot wheels cars, ride his back, push his son in the grocery store cart, play chasing games and hide-n-seek. Words
alone were not enough to help me understand the absence
of my daddy in those days. So I believed the only thing that
made sense in my little mind; *I'm just not good enough for
my dad to love me.*

The *Learning* Process
When I was six years old, I had to attend a Caucasian
school at the beginning few years of the country's integra-
tion of public schools. I was taught that being white was
good, being black was bad; being white was naturally intelligent, being black was inherently dumb. My mother made
me ride the "white" bus to begin learning about their race.
Oh, how I learned. I learned what it feels like to be called a
monkey though feeling like the ugly duckling on a bus full
of swans. I learned to stand in the middle of the aisle; my
arms tired from holding heavy books; my feet weary from
standing; the white students cringing as I approached their
seats. But during this tough time, God sent a little white

angel; one little brown haired, brown-eyed white girl who had mercy and let me share her seat. Alas, I got to rest my feet; no more bruises from falling over the edges of seats as the bus turned, and my little white angel got the fringe benefits of being called a monkey lover.

The next year, nothing had changed. The little white girl continued to save me a seat; the taunters continued to tease. Then one day- an epiphany! I saw a comic book picture of a Samurai warrior: strong arms wielding a sharp sword, sporting a vicious stare, and most of all protective armor. He was the greatest looking hero I had ever seen. He had the ability to fight and wield a sword like none other.

> *If the Samurai warrior was here, he could protect the little girl on the bus. Surely, if he were here, everyone being hurt would be saved. If he were here, everyone would be safe from mean people and bullies. I would be safe. Yea, heroes love the good guys and everyone loves a hero. Could the secret weapon of a hero be hidden inside him?* Something inside me wanted to know so desperately. *If I were a hero, then maybe my dad would love me.* Then an idea popped in my mind. *I would become the first black Samurai warrior. That was it!* So in my mind, I did.

I lived by miles and miles of woods. I secretly went into the woods and found a small hidden area and began building my Samurai warrior training ground. I stuffed old clothes and tied them on trees as my punching bags. I designed my very first Samurai warrior fighting suit from cut up blankets and large pants my sister thought she had lost.

Though I had most of the tools a training warrior could need, I had to forfeit one important training tool, country music. No fighter should train without his country music. Unfortunately, batteries did not power our family radio. Much to the despair of my neighbors, I had a peculiar fondness of the only style of music played on our local radio station. Each day after school I would open the windows in our African American neighborhood and fill the airwaves with the crème of country music!

Months after building my Samurai training ground, a black belt karate instructor opened a small karate school downtown. My mother agreed to let me join the small class. I was blown away with excitement when I saw all the weapons. There were swords, nunchaku (two sticks on a chain, pronounced "nunchucks,") and bo staffs (a stick more than 4ft long.) I was too small to begin learning the bo staff. I wanted to begin learning the sword, but the teacher would not let me. Maybe it was because he was unaware of my pursuit of Samurai greatness, or maybe he didn't want me to cut my legs off. I was left with one choice...to beat my head in each day while learning the nunchaku.

Samurai training did not lessen my troubles as I had originally presumed. It was quite the contrary. Since there were no opportunities for me to take advantage of schooling prior to first grade - the kindergarten program had not yet begun in my town - I was placed in the first grade class, which was full of white children with reading experience due to the privilege of having learning resources, which I did not. My inability to read only made my situation worse confining me to slow learning; and thereby more ridicule. This problem gave me an excuse to fight! A hero has to get practice fighting the bad guys, right? So I vowed to fight anyone who tried to hurt my friends or me.

Our teacher had a reputation for strictness. Simply put, she was downright mean! I will never forget my first attempt to read. My classmates were successfully reading their sentences out loud to the class. I was sitting in the very back of the classroom by the window. I hoped and prayed that she would not notice me, but of course, I was the least likely to be unnoticed. So, when she called on me to read, I could not read my sentence. A boy in the class saw an opportunity to humiliate me. He smiled an eerie smile at me. In my naivety, I tried to convince my mind: *Just maybe he was starting to like me and now wanted to be my friend. I mean look at him, he's giving me "thumbs up"...he wants to be my friend.* I felt a sense of hope in being accepted.

The teacher said to me, "See Spot run." Immediately, the boy pointed out the window and whispered to me, "Spot is a dog and he's running just outside your window." So I looked outside the window. The teacher raised her voice slightly to get my attention and repeated, "See Spot run." The boy again pointed out the window and whispered, "Don't you see Spot?" So I looked again. This time the teacher practically yelled at me, "Mr. Bradford...SEE SPOT RUN!" *Why was she yelling at me? Was I in trouble?* I responded in terror, "I can't see him. He must have ran by my window already." The whole class laughed uncontrollably. *Did that just happen? They are all laughing at me, because I am dumb and stupid.* These thoughts were overbearing to me. I had never felt so betrayed, hurt and ashamed. I wanted that feeling to go far away from me, but it stayed with me and got even stronger as they pointed and laughed at me. *Why won't they stop?* The teacher thought I was being sarcastic, so it was off to the Principal's office for me. *Why did she think I was being a bad boy?*

By this time, I was angry after suffering this betrayal. Upon seeing my *classroom helper*, I noticed that he was taunting other black children by calling them the "N" word. I had been looking for any reason to serve as hero and that was all I needed. As a black Samurai, I felt sworn to protect the honor of others. The fight was on! Every ounce of anger that had been building up inside me was going to be taken out on him. I kept thinking of all the taunting, the frowns, the betrayals, coarse jokes and laughing. My anger continued to rise uncontrollably as I witnessed his lethal weapon assassinating the character of others, and I just couldn't take it anymore. I ended up beating this kid to a pulp, and then it was back to the Principal's office again. It did not end there, however. Later, there was more injustice when I got on the bus. Another boy did something to embarrass the girl who saved me a seat each day. Yep, you got it! He was beaten down too. I felt that justice was served, and the innocent victims were avenged.

Now, my confidence had reached its peak, and I was more certain now than ever that I really could save the world as a mighty Samurai. Whenever spring of the year set in, my grandmama would warn me to not go in the woods. But she didn't realize that I *needed* to train harder at my secret training ground. My mother would work late at the Acme Boot Company. Grandmama was a janitor at the high school and cleaned parts of the building long after my sister and I came home. Plenty of housewives in our neighborhood would periodically watch the kids who were alone due to working guardians, and I knew what time they would come to our house. I was certain I could sneak off to the woods without anyone knowing.

Fight or Flight

One day, I persuaded a neighbor girl to go with me to the Samurai training ground and watch me practice fighting. She was afraid that the Japanese would find out that I was trying to be a black Samurai. She just didn't know what I knew. The way of the Samurai was to accept any worthy warrior for training regardless of race. And besides that, they would be honored to have a black Samurai. In another obvious state of apprehension, she reminded me that my grandmother said not to go in the woods, yet she was lured by the top-secret nature of the concealed camp. We walked through the blankets of underbrush and thickets of trees covering the hidden spot where I trained. *Ah, there it was!*

Something was different that day. As I trudged with excitement toward the hideout, I stepped on something coiled and rubbery. Out of nowhere, I felt something pointed and sharp suddenly pierce my leg just above my ankle. *Ouch!* I looked down, and to my great surprise it was a large snake- coiled to strike again. "Let's get out of here!" my friend yelped as she dashed away. Her face depicted sheer horror, but at the same time concern for me. I panicked and hopped away from the angry viper, fearing it would bite me again. After catching up, my friend and I walked back home. At the time, I was unaware of the immense danger I was in from the venomous bite, so my thoughts turned to who would save *my* butt from the inevitable fate at the hands of my grandmama, yet I was still in pain. *I need a hero. Where is my hero?* Gradually, the poison penetrated my nervous system. After sitting on a wooden log in the back yard, I assured my friend that I was all right. Likewise, unaware of the danger she left to go home.

Nearly an hour later, I still sat on the log, but now I could hardly feel my body from the waist down. My leg now resembled a rubber balloon and inflated more and more as the minutes passed. The poignant pain and the redness of my skin caused me to wonder if I were going to die. *Samurais don't go out like this, why am I so weak? What's going to happen to all the hurt people if I die?* The mother next door looked over at me from her back porch and noticed my unusual distress. As she came closer she saw my swollen leg. She was petrified when she saw the fang holes in my leg. I looked at her face as it revealed her thoughts. "She thinks I'm going to die," I thought feeling my heart pound harder and faster. Barely awake, I feel her drag me to the front porch of her house. She screams for my mother who is now at home. The next thing I remember is nurses and doctors and the pain of two shots sticking me in the butt on a cold hospital table.

I heard the doctor saying how amazed he was to see a child survive this long without treatment from such a devastating snakebite. He too did not think that I would survive. I overheard him ask my mother to see my dad. *Oh, doctors must see other dad's coming to be with their sick children. Maybe I will get to see my dad now.* Following the request for my dad, I heard an intense fiery dialogue on the phone between my mother and father, who was in another city. By the look on her face, I knew my dad was not coming.

As I lay almost motionless in the hospital bed, my grandmother sat beside me. The throbbing area around the snakebite felt like sharp pins pricking my leg. It hurt badly. Incoherent at times the pain felt like someone had taken a match and set my whole body on fire. The doctors and nurses did not expect me to live. My grandmother understood me and showed great compassion as she looked into my eyes. I could feel such strength from her, yet a soft peace. If she feared for my life, she never revealed it to me. The pain in my body took a back seat to the pain in my heart as she sat there listening as my heart poured out questions: "Why doesn't my daddy love me? Will I someday be a good daddy? Will you help me save the world? Am I going to die?" She just smiled and ignored my near death state, but she told me things that she reminded me of later:

> Son, you ain't going nowhere right now. Some people are marked to die. You are marked to live. This won't be the first time that God saved you from dying and probably not the last. Your mother was pregnant with you in her tummy and just about ready to give birth to you. One dark night she got this terrible pain in her side. She started

vomiting all over the house and fell hard on the floor. She couldn't get up. Son, all I knew to do was to pray and call my brother who had a car. The closest hospital turned us down because they didn't take colored women who were about to have a baby. So we drove all the way to the colored hospital. Come to find out, yo' mama's appendix had busted. Now, they said only nine times ever had both the mama and the baby lived through this type of thing, but son, we believe in prayer, 'cause prayer sho'nough changes things. I don't care what nobody says, it was a miracle you both survived. So you just have faith right now. In the mighty name of Jesus, you ain't going nowhere. You gonna keep on going to church every Sunday like you been taught to do. You gonna get your education, 'cause a man ain't nothing without an education. You gonna learned that karate stuff cause ain't nobody ever gonna run over you. You gonna be much more than me or anybody around here, cause you gonna be a man of God with love in your heart for everybody. So go to sleep son. You ain't going nowhere.

Though my earthly daddy didn't show up, my grand-mama let me know my heavenly Father was right by my side. As I was falling asleep in anticipation, I quietly announced, "Grandmama, I have to tell you a secret. I am the first black Samurai."

Chapter 2

ALL AMERICAN BOY

A wise man in history once said, "A man's gift makes room for him and brings him before great men." The man's name was Solomon. Actually, he was the wisest man that ever lived before Christ walked the earth. From kindergarten through fifth grade, I thought my gift was to beat up bad guys. After all, I was Samurai Joe. Unfortunately, once you beat up a few guys in grade school, you earn every one's respect and there's no reason to fight anymore. Still experiencing a deep feeling of unworthiness from the absence of my father, I needed to add another notch on my belt to my reputation to demonstrate that even without a dad I could be as good as anyone.

My First Love

By my sixth grade year, the racial climate had changed considerably as any student could try out for junior high sports peaceably. Regrettably, I was short and didn't quite measure up to play basketball, and in my assessment, being crushed by overgrown eighth graders on the football field did not seem logical to a Samurai like me. Surprisingly, something other than sports caught my attention. One day as I walked by the band room, the sound of the music fascinated me to the point of enticing me towards it. *Wow, that sound is coming from kids? Could I be a part of that?*

A warm fuzzy feeling stirred within me; it touched my soul. I had found my first love.

Hanging on the entrance door of the band room, a large sign stated: "Sixth Grade Band Sign-up." Inside the band room were all sorts of instruments, but it was the trumpet that caught my attention. I made a mental decision that I would choose it figuring with only three valves, it would be easier to master than the other instruments. When I got home, my mother was excited about my musical interests, but she wanted me to play the saxophone. I said "Saxo... what?!" The name even made it seem hard to play, besides it had too many little buttons on it to learn.

The next day, I told the middle-aged white band instructor that I wanted to play the trumpet. As to not embarrass me in front of the other students, he leaned in and quietly told me something that at first felt like a slap in the face. He whispered, "Your lips are entirely too big to play the trumpet. You would probably advance faster on the saxophone." I felt a little embarrassed and ashamed of my lips. *My ugly lips are keeping me from the instrument I like. Is he being mean to me, too? Is he really trying to help?* I couldn't figure it out. I didn't know whether to call the NAACP or to thank him. It didn't matter, because I felt so special going home with a shiny instrument in my hand. I was exuberant with joy. I, Joe Bradford, was holding something of value and worth. I felt so privileged, because I was trusted. I imagined my mama smiling from cheek to cheek, welling up with happiness and delight over my choosing the instrument that she wanted me to play. When I told her what the band instructor said to me, she just laughed. *What have I gotten myself into now? There are so many buttons. Would I even be able to learn this thing?* Turns out it was wonderful advice to play the saxophone—I enjoyed it.

First Stage of Success

Early success on the saxophone brought unexpected attention toward me. I was being graced with something that did not hurt people. It seemed that music was indeed the language of the world. I could feel something inside me changing, something new and totally different. One day an old rival bumped into me in the hallway. My first reaction was to KICK HIS..., but something strange came out of my mouth. I said, "Look man, I'm sorry. I wasn't watching where I was going. See you later." Then I just walked away feeling very weird, but good inside. My rival had a smile of appreciation on his face toward me—a genuine one—for the first time. I was completely shocked! This was the same guy who betrayed me with a phony smile in first grade. Now he was sincerely smiling at me. I was in a daze of amazement thinking about the irony of that. Even though it felt strange, I actually liked the new me that was finally rising up. After getting home and telling my grandmother the turn of events, she said, "They both work, but you can gather more flies with honey than the backside of a horse." The simple lesson was being nice is always better. Mama's words encouraged me to embrace my first love and my now second love, being nice. And so it was that at the end of the sixth grade year, I came in first place in the class solo competition with many friends congratulating me afterwards.

My Greatest Gift

During junior high my popularity increased. Unknown to me at the time, travelling the road of humility set me on course to be graced with my greatest gift: versatility. The overwhelming drive to adapt to any situation became my mission.

This mission inspired me to study successful white students' academic excellence. The first trait of successful white students that stood out to me was their attendance records. I noticed that the best students rarely missed class. So I adapted....I mean really adapted! I decided to make a change in my attendance, which was huge for me. After the sixth grade, I never missed a day of school again. My scrapbook shows that upon graduating from high school, I received a perfect attendance certificate for six consecutive years of school. I was proud of that.

The old saying, "Nice guys finish last" is not always the truth. Since I liked the feeling of being loved by everyone so much, I was determined to be nice to everyone, like a hero should. At the eighth grade banquet, I was the first black male in our school's history to be honored by the teachers with the Citizenship Award. It was my finest moment. I felt noticed, accepted and loved from the collective body of students and teachers. Despite this, I realized that being likable did not improve my grades, so by the end of Junior high my grades were only average. This was not acceptable to me; I made up in my mind to conform academically as well. That nagging feeling nudging me to prove my worthiness was still silently eating away at me, so, I felt compelled to prove once and for all that I was indeed respectable and important, by being smart and making good grades. *Maybe then I will be good enough for my dad to love me,* I thought, trying to convince myself. So, to adapt academically in high school, I made the wisest and most obvious decision...to study the nerds!

My Inner Nerd

Upon entering high school, astigmatism had formed in my eyes causing me to require glasses—huge, black, ugly ones. This was perfect! Now I even looked like a nerd. My grades were bound to improve now! I met a white boy and fellow nerd named John, who was a transfer from another little town. He also played saxophone. Now, there are serious nerds, and there are silly nerds. Thank God, John was a silly nerd. We became close friends. He was not just any nerd. He was destined to become the geometry champ of the entire state of Tennessee. In short, he was like a mathematical genius. I yearned to be smart like him, so I observed his ways and learned from studying him. I became the first black boy in our county to become a member of the Mu Alpha Theta Mathematics Club, another highlight in my scrapbook.

Nobody knew that secretly in the back of my mind, there was still residue to prove to the world that I was good regardless of my dad leaving me. This drive would even override my mission to overcome racial stereotypes of African Americans being less intelligent. In this moment, my foremost pursuit was to complete the total package of student excellence demonstrating that success is possible without a dad in sight. So I studied additional successful white students. Just as in present-day educational arena, success was measured then by the grades one obtained. Good grades would reap an even greater sign of success, college scholarships. Going to college meant you were really bound for great success Everybody in my neighborhood believed that. That was all I heard from my culture, *if you go to college you are somebody! You are going to be important.* Besides, a tiny voice in my mind would always remind me what my grandmama said to me in the hospital, "You gonna get your education, cause a man ain't nothing without an education." I was 13 years old at the time, and though I yearned for scholasticism; I would not sacrifice "cool" to achieve it. Being "cool" took athleticism.

From Geek to Jock

In the seventies, Bruce Lee popularized karate, and many a young person spent countless hours watching his movies and admiring his skills; I was one of them. His weapon of choice in the movies was the nunchaku. *Yes, all the years of beating myself in the head with the nunchaku had finally paid off!* I had mastered it. Swinging the nunchaku rapidly was now as natural as walking down the street. So training in martial arts meant instant "cool" points for me, Samurai Joe.

Yet, I was not satisfied with that niche. I felt compelled to deliver a total package of athleticism at school, which meant also lettering in a sport. As time progressed, I became well known throughout the county for making All Star Teams in Little League Baseball from age eight through high school. Once a sophomore, I easily made the varsity baseball team. As a junior, I was awarded the Most Improved Player of the Year trophy with the team's second highest batting average. It felt rewarding to make my coach happy and proud of me. *Was this what having a father was like?* My uttermost thoughts were focused on making my absent father proud of his athletic son; I wondered if he would have been.

All State Competition

The grace of musical talent took a leap in high school. I failed terribly in the Fall 1977 Mid State Band competition try-outs. This feeling of defeat was all too familiar, and I didn't like the memories it evoked. So I made a game plan; I was determined to beat the odds. Mr. Versatility was also Mr. Resilient. I bounced back quickly, overcoming failure by observing the style and techniques of the competition's winners. My lofty ambitions led me to an unheard of decision to compete the following year on both alto and tenor saxophones. My hopes were to increase my odds of securing *any* seat in the Mid State Band. Over the year, I did three things to prepare myself: I practiced, practiced, and then practiced. I didn't have much, but I had something that couldn't be taken from me—hope.

The following summer my mother allowed me to go to a private jazz camp at University of Tennessee, Chattanooga. This camp had only great players, with the slight exception of me, but this would serve to be a pivotal experience in my musical skill. I received motivation from the influence of my super-talented white peers; because they played so great, it made me want to do the same. The thing that impacted me the most was being trained by the director himself. I had never seen anyone play saxophone like him. He was incredible! Someone that great was supporting and encouraging me in ways I had always wanted from a male figure. He made me feel loved and worthy of his time. This was so awesome! This was a dream come true. I knew then, my love for music became more intimate.

In the fall of 1978, my senior year, I competed for a spot at the Mid State Band try-outs on both alto and tenor saxophones. The entire competition was tense, as out of the more than 100 people auditioning on my instruments, only eight would be chosen for the Mid-State band for alto sax and only six for tenor sax. To add to the anxiety, only the top two performers on alto sax, and one performer on tenor sax would be chosen for the esteemed All State Band. My strongest competition on tenor saxophone was the current reigning All State champion. It was doubted that anyone could even come close to defeating him for the only All State position.

The tradition at the time was to dress nicely for the competition, though the judges were behind a screen and could not see the contestants. My family was very poor, and I had out grown my clothes, which made my securing attire for the event, an uncomfortable situation. This was a difficult and humbling time for me, as I had nowhere else to turn but to my cousin who offered me some old pants and a faded sports jacket. *I must fit in and look important so they will accept me.* Upon dressing, I surmised that nothing about my attire exemplified success; my clothes were unattractive and the heels on my shoes were run down. Pulling myself out of these thoughts, I regained perspective: Clothes had nothing to do with my ability to play the saxophone.

The first competition was the alto saxophone. All my

summer job money for three years had gone toward purchasing a high quality alto saxophone with the sweetest tone ever created. The competition on alto sax was stiff with so many great players. I felt so little and insignificant. I wanted to be chosen for this band and I stirred up enough courage to stand straight with my chin up regardless of how I felt inside. My stomach was in a knot. My heart was throbbing with anticipation. I had never been so nervous.

Then it was time to compete on the tenor saxophone. I didn't own a tenor saxophone, so I had been practicing all year on an old one owned by the school. The reigning tenor saxophone champion played great as expected with the exception of one note at the end of the music piece. I played shortly after him and the crowd had left. Only a few people were by the door listening. I felt the intense loneliness of no one being in my corner to win. To muster up enough faith to compete it was necessary to forget the skill of the reigning champ as well as all the other great players. When I left the try-out room, the hallway was surprisingly full again. It was quite embarrassing. I thought I did ok.

At the end of the whole competition, everyone waited for the judge's rulings. They came out of the boardroom whispering with strange looks on their faces. My faith lowered substantially as I noticed all the well-dressed white students around me. Then alarm pierced my soul as the judges walked directly toward me. I was overtaken by fear. Was I disqualified for wearing poor clothing? Were they going to embarrass me in front of everyone to make an example of me?

The closer the judges came the more they began to grin. I just knew they were going to enjoy tormenting me by singling me out from the white competitors. The head judge stepped right in front of me and asked me to stand in front of the crowd. Even the security guards were there to watch. Terrifying thoughts filled my head. The head judge then addressed the crowd and said, "For the first time in Mid-State band history…" …*I knew this was it…me, the African American black boy who couldn't afford proper attire would be arrested…my mother and grandmother would see me in jail on the Six O'clock News.* "…a student has won All State positions on both alto and tenor saxophone!"

My heart almost exploded in shock! Tears began to well up in my eyes. The moment was almost too overwhelming for me. *What? No! Both? Me? Huh???* Since no human can play two horns at the same time, in two separate music sections, I chose alto saxophone as my All State position. The former reigning tenor sax champ was even excited. He had come in second place and took my position as the All State tenor sax representative. *Unbelievable!* The All State competition results with my picture holding both an alto and tenor saxophone made our county newspaper, which is another highlight in my scrapbook. I thought maybe, just maybe, my dad would have loved to see the newspaper article.

Scholastic Achievement Scrapbook

Both the black and white communities were forced to take note as I graduated as one of the most decorated students of any race in my town's history. Having ranked in the top 10% of my graduating class, my plan of studying successful white students had worked perfectly, and afforded me the additional benefit of true friendship with them and immense popularity all around. The student body had elected me, a once ridiculed and humiliated black boy, as Vice President of Student Council *and* Vice President of my senior class.

Other achievements in my scrapbook include, Beta Club Honor Society, Who's Who Among High School Students, and a nomination for Boy's State. Also in my senior year, the teachers chose me for the "Citizenship Award" among all my peers and placed my name on a plaque displayed in the school's historical award case from that day to present. This honor came four years after the same award by different teachers. My scrapbook also contains a newspaper article that shows my favorite recognition of all chosen by my peers…"Most Versatile." *How could all of this be possible without a father's affirmation or approval? I abandoned my quest to impress my father, and took on a new one of proving that I didn't need him.*

Scholarship Recruiters

Upon graduating High School, life could not get any sweeter, or at least I thought. Universities all over the state and beyond were "courting" me with full music scholarships, and somehow the University of Tennessee, Knoxville learned of my scholastic success and sent an engineering scholarship recruiter to my school. After an interview, he took my application and went back to Knoxville to have his board evaluate me.

Music was my first love, but my new love now was more money, which was the reward of a degree in any branch of engineering (a prominent choice of studies during that time.) Mixed emotions of excitement and fear gripped me, as I deduced that this would be the final key to unlock the doors to complete success.

Meanwhile, my saxophone trainer from the Chattanooga Jazz Camp called tempting me with an offer to do a summer tour with him in Europe. It was an all expense paid opportunity to simultaneously receive top-dollar compensation as a young musician and increase my skills. This experience would be a fun way to greatly propel my musical career. My family, however, was hoping for a positive response from the engineering scout before I chose the summer music tour in Europe.

Chosen for College

Soon after the European trip offer, the verdict came back from the University of Tennessee. They had chosen me and only 56 other students from throughout the country to be awarded a "full" (all expense paid) cooperative engineering scholarship. This program included completing seven three-month training sessions at Eastman Kodak, the state's largest chemical company at the time, and be awarded an unbelievable compensation. How could this be? They were essentially paying me to go to college and to gain experiential knowledge in my field. Then the gravy; a scholarship awarded by my home county's University of Tennessee Alumni group, the Alumni Freshman Scholarship, would make me a "rich" freshman. The offer was simply too good to pass up. This whole agreement was placed proudly in my scrapbook that I keep even today as a reminder of the height of the early climb to success. This scrapbook would show anyone—by anyone, I mean my father—that I had worth.

All American Boy

Now you see. My goal was secured…my mission accomplished. I personified the All American boy! Absolutely everyone in my town could see that I graduated king of the mountain. Nobody could name one person from my high school, black or white, with more accomplishments. In the words of my nearly illiterate grandmother, "You couldn't tell me nothin'." College would be a breeze. The American dream was only a taste away.

My short and long term goals were etched. I would use my college cooperative experience to make money, save money, buy a car, and impress the ladies. Then I would graduate at the top of my engineering class, operate a large engineering firm ten years after graduating, and most of all, finally prove my worth to the world. I was an independent and accomplished man, without a father figure. All my achievements were not inherently bad, but my issues of abandonment had opened the door to self-importance, arrogance, and callousness. This self-importance masked the true feelings of pain I had in my heart, and I thought it protected me from dwelling and living in that pain. My ego welcomed this condition of heightened significance, but my soul cried out from the damage. I thought that if I could achieve things on my own without the need of my father, I would truly be great. This pain inside me would finally cease. I would prove to myself that my ambition alone was enough to succeed in life.

Have you ever had seasons of success when you forgot that you didn't do anything great alone? Solomon not only spoke of a man's gifts, he also spoke of the consequences of pride. Without a heart of humility, I didn't realize that I was losing the grace that empowered great feats. Of course, "Humpty Dumpty" had to first sit on a wall before he had a great fall. Without my knowledge, I was on a collision course to reproof.

Chapter 3

ORIGINAL HACKER CLUB

There are stages of life where every human is forced to face drastic changes. Attending college far away from home is one of those experiences for many people. At the age of seventeen, it was time for me to leave the nest. Adult decisions had to happen quickly as the excitement of freedom from parental rule boiled like hot water inside of me. In the final days of home life, I could hardly wait to leave town. My teachers had drilled in me that a machine called a computer would someday define the information age and was quickly on the rise. Whatever power the computer held for success, I had no doubt in my mind that I would master it, or would it master me?

The perks of the fabulous cooperative scholarship program began before my high school graduation date. My principal gave me a letter of exemption from my last week of school to attend the special University of Tennessee, Knoxville (UTK) freshman training camp for students in the engineering scholarship program. Although I returned the day before the Sunday graduation ceremony, I looked forward to the next week. *Freedom!* Each of the 57 students in the program were sent to various companies all over the country, and I was off to Eastman Kodak in Kingsport, TN, which was over 300 miles from home, for the entire summer.

Computer Training 101

Eastman Kodak was like a small city. Thousands of employees flocked there every day. How could a college student make so much money before even setting a foot in a classroom? Unaccustomed to being noticed for my good looks, I warmly welcomed the female's attention that money brought. Handsome or ugly, I was a hot commodity for any small town cowgirl who could lasso me in, and believe me, they tried. The good life was advancing along as I was introduced on my first day to the tool that would shape my destiny: a computer. At that time, the computer was called a "mainframe" and it filled a large room in another building of the company. Employees would access the mainframe computer through what was called a computer terminal. A computer terminal looked sort of like a desktop personal computer of today, but the terminal was simply a device to communicate to the mainframe computer. My job did not require programming the computer, only operating it. The entire summer at Eastman Kodak was spent keeping track of warehouse inventory on the computer. Everything I learned there was interesting to me, so I seized every moment as an opportunity to gain knowledge.

To a small town boy entering the state's largest university, college life was a world of wonders and distraction such as football, parties and girls. However, my scholastic success was not compromised. In fact, of all of the scholarship recipients, only twelve of us made the Dean's List in the first Fall Quarter of college. The publicity of this award from the scholarship department unfortunately caused more conceit to grow in my heart, though it was veiled with false humility. I was good and I knew it.

Then came time for my first computer programming class, Basic. The time conflict of pledging one of the school's most popular black fraternities caused me to do poorly in the class. Did this hinder my quest for computer greatness? Not at all! It only increased my drive to master the computer. Understand that defeat was not an option within me. The next school year, I took the Basic programming language again and made an "A" in the class.

Computer Hacking 101

After completing my freshman year in college, my cooperative schedule until the senior year was as follows: Summer and Winter quarters were paid work training at Eastman Kodak, while Fall and Spring quarters were study at UTK. One quarter I was scheduled to work in Eastman Kodak's computer department with the systems manager, for which a Fortran (the primary engineering and mathematical programming language) class was a prerequisite. In spite of not having taken it yet, I was allowed to work there based on my previous success in Basic.

An incredible thing happened during this work period. In just a few short weeks I had astonishingly learned the Fortran language from self-study in a book. The ability to program pages of computer codes for Eastman's Yarn plant, greatly impressed the computer department employees, nevertheless, no one was more impressed than me. I programmed day and night. I felt like a robot had been turned on in my head. I wondered what on earth was happening to me. *How could this be possible?* The ease of programming was literally freaking me out.

Then the previous gift of adapting reignited. Studying the Systems Manager became my most important quest. He was my personal project. He not only was a master programmer, but he was also the troubleshooter. He knew absolutely everything about the mainframe computer. In the 1970's and early 1980's the term "mainframe computer" was almost synonymous with IBM due to their national market share. Therefore, almost every company and every university in the country used an IBM mainframe. Learning how the IBM mainframe worked was an entirely different animal and became my obsession. It was obvious to me that everyone in Eastman Kodak, using a computer terminal, was dependent on the Systems Manager of the IBM mainframe.

No job could truly claim "king of the mountain" as much as the Systems Manager's position. He controlled the IBM mainframe, which was the most rare and possibly greatest intelligence in the company. To me, he was "the goose that laid the golden egg." I became his shadow, watching and following him everywhere in the company. As ingenious as he was, he was very shy and few people took time to talk with him. He was a classic nerd, just my cup of tea. I loved nerds. I questioned and watched him unceasingly, and yet he never knew what I was up to.

After completing the work quarter with the Systems Manager, I easily excelled in the Fortran programming class at UTK. I later took Pascal, which was one of the primary business programming languages. The word got around that I could program exceptionally in various computer languages, and the Minority Student Affairs Office paid me to tutor other college students. My popularity for programming was spreading, and my ego inflated with it. Unknown to others, programming computer languages was not the extent of my knowledge. I knew the computer system itself.

What a Hack!

In the early 1980's, the term "computer hacking" was gaining popularity. One day I just decided to do it; I began to hack. By now, I knew the IBM mainframe computer very well; most of all, I knew its weaknesses. Success in hacking depended on weaknesses that others did not know. UTK's IBM mainframe Systems Manager probably knew the same weaknesses. There was little the Systems Manager could do if someone knowledgeable of the system broke in. The so-called "firewalls" like we have today to block a potential hacker did not exist. There were multiple vulnerabilities in the IBM mainframes of the time, and I knew most of them.

So it began. There were hundreds of computer terminals on UTK's large campus. Computer terminal labs were in the dorms, libraries, classroom buildings, the University Center, and in virtually every part of the campus. I easily hacked into various areas of UTK's mainframe through different computer terminals never using the same terminal twice. I had at least enough dignity to never break one primary rule, no hacking into the grade archive. However, dropping and adding classes was a whole different thing. I felt there needed to be a little justice in the system as it pertained to teachers — some were more strict, some boring, and others overly difficult. It just did not make sense to me to be anguished in classes with these types of professors. With a little bit of hacking at the beginning of the school quarter, the most desired teachers became my teachers. And yes, I did give a handful of close friends the benefit of prized teachers, and my wrath came against a handful of rival fraternity leaders by placing them in the classrooms of undesirable teachers. The power of the whole university being at my mercy was invigorating during this time.

At Eastman Kodak, I had learned how to set up terminals and switch the codes. There was a way to send a deceptive diversion to not only hide oneself, but also simultaneously incriminating someone else to take the blame if necessary. Playing cat and mouse with the UTK systems manager and UTK security became a dangerously fun past time. At times I would leave the classic signature of hackers, "CATCH ME IF YOU CAN! CATCH ME IF YOU CAN! CATCH ME IF YOU CAN..." scrolling down the computer terminal screen.

What the Hack?

The arrogance of hacking was becoming irresistible to me. News reports were being released more and more on teenagers and college students growing a secret hacking society. A smart computer hacker would never reveal his actual identity openly, but he would at times make his existence known to other hackers. An awful disease grew in my mind to be the best, so I took a dare to hack into a local bank. To access money, the dare included getting funds from an Automatic Teller Machine (ATM). This process would require getting someone's ATM card, hacking into the bank's mainframe and getting their secret ATM code, then testing the code out with the card at an actual ATM.

Thoughts of secret agent status filled my head. I was caught in a fantasy where reality had no meaning. I knew just whose ATM card to secretly "borrow", an unsuspecting classmate who shared a class project with me. His card was easy to acquire. Not totally expecting to be able to win the dare, I found a way to get into the bank's mainframe. Once inside the mainframe it took little work to locate the file with the ATM codes. As I scanned through the file, I noticed that the names were neatly alphabetized. I then came across my classmate's secret code.

I visited a local ATM machine one night to try the code. To my surprise, it worked! No local hacker could stake their claim to this one. I had done it! It was woefully ignorant that the intense reality of intellectual power had blinded me, but the hidden camera on the ATM machine was not blinded. Then the next day my classmate also noticed money was missing in his account, and so was his card! He reported the lost card to the bank. The bank had my picture on file on the night of the ATM transaction. I was so busted!

When the police detective called me, I freely went to the UTK police department to turn myself in. Once I arrived, those familiar feelings of humiliation taunted me once again: *I am so stupid. How could I be so stupid?* Oh, the shame that flooded my mind! This time I must admit my feelings were true, but I did not want to go to jail for a stupid $200 dare.

The detective held my wrist tightly and took me to the police car to transport me to the city jail. In a moment of great panic and stupidity I used my Samurai skills and broke loose from the detective and ran, hoping I didn't hurt his hand too badly. I was so afraid that I just lost it! I ran so fast that the detective and other policemen were unable to catch me.

I went to a fraternity brother's apartment hiding out from the police who were in pursuit. I could hear propellers of helicopters flying around the campus. I imagined enraged police officers, grasping their weapons, probing the campus grounds for the culprit that had just assaulted their partner. Was I trapped in some kind of action packed motion picture? What in the world had I done?

My fraternity brother and I came up with a strategy of escape. He was a hefty guy who worked out daily. I got in a duffel bag, and he threw me on his back like a small sack of potatoes. He walked out to his car inconspicuously, and situated me in the trunk. As I heard his door slam and felt the car begin to roll, it was then that my dread truly hit. I could see no light as I laid in this duffel bag in a curled position. The ride in that dim trunk was the longest and most nerve-wrecking and terrifying ride I've ever taken. It had given me more than enough time to think about the drama in my life. Agonizing thoughts flooded my mind:

Oh my God...this cannot be happening. Am I going to be marked as a dangerous criminal? How am I going to live a life on the run now? I have to figure this out. What have I done? Everyone will ridicule me now. What will people say about me? I wasn't trying to harm anyone. What will my punishment be? This is all my fault...I am to blame for the pending treatment awaiting me. God please don't abandon me now. I know I have been bad, but PLEASE don't leave me now! It's so dark in here. Where are we now? Are we almost there?

Lying in the trunk, I could see a little tiny dim light through a hole of the trunk. We traveled far from the university to a town just inside of the Kentucky border. Crazy! I then caught a bus and traveled far, far away from Knoxville to the home of a childhood friend in Dallas, Texas. She was the daughter of my old pastor back at home. I stayed there for two days. It just so happened that her live-in boyfriend had previously been in trouble with the law and he convinced me to turn right around and travel back to Knoxville to face the court because it wasn't worth living a life on the run.

I took his advice and traveled back. When I walked inside the university police department, this time the detective put handcuffs on me immediately. Needless to say, the detective did not appreciate me hurting his arm when I broke away from him a few days earlier. The way they treated me was a reminder of my childhood years at school. I felt like a hardened criminal at the mercy of policemen who wanted revenge on me. *Were they going to take a back road and beat me? Were they going to make an example out of me to the other policemen?* Chaotic thoughts like this plagued my mind. I felt somewhat safe when I saw the downtown jailhouse. My mother sent money for bail, and I got out of jail. There are no words that can express the shame and dishonor I felt for being a disappointment to my grandmama and mother.

Terror gripped me to the core of my inner being. *How would the judge punish me?* Peaceful sleep ceased to exist for days. I was sent to two different places for discipline to take place, the state judge and the college disciplinary board. The college disciplinary judge noticed that I was a member of the National Engineering Honor Society, a 4.0 GPA student during that quarter and an upperclassman. The college disciplinary judge gave me probation allowing me to stay in school. The State of Tennessee, on the other hand, would not let me off so easy. When I went in front of the judge in court, he gave me a year to complete my engineering degree without placing any sentence on me.

I was haunted the entire last year of college with thoughts of incarceration, but my life began to seemingly take a turn for the better when I began the job interview process. At the time, I had completed the full cooperative program at Eastman Kodak through four years of going from UTK to Eastman and back to UTK every three months. My experience and grades qualified me to interview with some of the nations most successful engineering and computer companies. The school officials were nearly certain that the judge would let me off with probation. Life was somewhat great again, and I stopped nearly all computer hacking.

It was my final quarter at UTK. I took an overload of classes to ensure I would graduate in the summer quarter. I got sick and missed a couple final exams, largely from the emotional stress of having to go before the judge in a couple of weeks. Pressure in my heart stressed my whole body as I had muscle aches, chest pains and extreme exhaustion. My plan was to march at the graduation ceremony and take the remaining two final exams, which were scheduled for two weeks later.

I did march with my class but would not receive my diploma until after taking the final exams. Moments after the graduation ceremony, my classmates and friends talked about the great job offers we had received. My moment of success had finally come to its fruition. We discussed new cars, marriage, and finally living the American dream we all had worked so hard for. IBM had offered me a highly lucrative job just outside of Washington, DC, where I had recently visited and interviewed. IBM was the dream job at the time and the job all my peers envied. I was scheduled for court the week in between graduation ceremony and my last two final exams. I was all set to head to IBM two weeks following the finals.

The day inescapably came to see the criminal judge. I had hoped all the years of hard work, all the hours spent studying, and all the accolades I had built up would surely count for something. The judge had allowed me to stay out of jail to complete my final year of college. *Surely this burden hanging over my head would be all over after today.* The judge's first words seemed to confirm that I would be let off with a "slap on the wrist." He acknowledged my accomplishments in college, my hard work, and my history in helping others through tutoring, yet unexpectedly the judge's words began to morph. Though my college leaders and peers believed I would remain free, one important fact was still hanging over my head. The criminal authorities never knew *how* I was able to get my classmates secret code.

The judge knew of public events like the movie *Wargames,* which glamorized computer hacking. He knew computer hacking was multiplying suspicion with the state and federal governments. Computer hacking was creating a criminal war and unfortunately for me, I was now considered the enemy. He gave me a look that caused me to freeze in my seat. I could hear a tiny voice in my mind whisper, *"No."* Regardless of my accomplishments, he felt compelled to send me to jail and use my punishment as an example.

In the midst of his statements, he mentioned a prank incident a couple of years earlier in which I was involved as a fraternity leader. We had mischievously switched furniture between several apartments and even sold some. The case had been filed as a pretrial diversion and would have been soon taken off my record if I had stayed out of trouble. Well, silly me, I didn't stay out of trouble. This was the judge's ticket to give me plenty of jail time. The pretrial diversion was dropped and the charges associated with the prank incident were made active again. Though I was not directly caught computer hacking, the result of my supposedly ingenious hacking abilities had indirectly caused me to be sentenced to jail for eight years. I would be required to fulfill thirty percent of the sentence minus time off for good behavior and other time credits.

As the judge raised, then smashed his gavel upon his desk in judgment, I felt like that gavel physically reached toward me and seized every dream that I labored on and every goal that I had set my entire life. It placed my helpless life beneath its power and crushed it into a million tiny irreconcilable pieces. Time in my world stood still for a moment. I could physically do nothing. I saw myself standing in front of an ATM machine, pompously holding a meager $200 in my hand and wearing a proud smirk. If I could just turn back the hands of time. If I could just erase that whole day...

I came out of this devastating state only to feel my arms being snatched up and locked together by two pitiless officers. As they drug me away, I found myself violently fighting my lungs to catch my next breath. It felt like all air in that room had been sucked away and I was suffocating.

Immensely distraught, I was taken away by the guards in unimaginable despair. As I was being taken away I pictured in my mind the heartache of my grandmama and mother screaming out for mercy. I pictured the destiny of all my friends without me. Mentally, I chronicled my friends leaving in their cars, happily arriving at their jobs, happily buying their homes, and later happily married with children. *What would life hold for me now? How could a college boy survive where I was headed?* I cried out inside for the first time, *"Please God, forgive me! Please help me!"* How *would I ever be of use to anybody now? How would anybody ever care for or love me?* I had failed in a monumental way. Even if I survived, I would be marked with the stigma of having gone to prison. My bed of destruction was made, and I now had to lie in it. The mountain that my pride had built all came tumbling down on top of me at once. I was left with one word to God... *"Please."*

Chapter 4

WOLF OR SHEEP!

"Then the King will say to those on His right hand, 'Come, you blessed of My Father, inherit the kingdom prepared for you from the foundation of the world: for I was hungry and you gave Me food; I was thirsty and you gave Me drink; I was a stranger and you took Me in; I was naked and you clothed Me; I was sick and you visited Me; <u>I was in prison and you came to Me.</u>'

Then the righteous will answer Him, saying, 'Lord, when did we see You hungry and feed You, or thirsty and give You drink? When did we see You a stranger and take You in, or naked and clothe You? Or when did we see You sick, or in prison, and come to You?' And the King will answer and say to them, 'Assuredly, I say to you, inasmuch as you did it to one of the least of these My brethren, you did it to Me.'" (Matthew 25:34-40)

Have you ever had a time in life where you felt as if doom hovered over your head like a dark cloud? Many people can counsel you on how to climb mountains of success in various areas of life, but what happens when it seems like you have fallen into a pit of failure that tarnishes all light in your reputation? Misery from watching my whole life's accomplishments being crushed dominated my thinking. Without fraternity brothers watching my back, and the solace of the college security department at my "beck and call", and without a friend in sight, I felt like a sheep being led to the slaughter, and it was all my fault. Nevertheless, in prison, one of the darkest places on earth, I was on a path to meet ambassadors of Christ. And so it all began. . . .

Intake "Drunk Tank"

As guards took me away from normal life, I was not able to return to my campus apartment to pack my bags. All of "my personal possessions" lay dormant where I left them outside the jail walls. If no friend or family member packed and stored my clothes, then apartment security would auction it off or throw it away. My car had to be driven from the courthouse or be towed and sold. I no longer owned anything. I was now the property of the State of Tennessee. They changed my name to a number that I had to quickly remember and listen attentively for or be left out when medication or other necessities were brought in. The only basic right I had was to live, though at times even life itself would have to be won. I could only ponder these words: *How low have I fallen?*

Anxiety of the unknown rose in my heart as I approached the Knox County Intake Cell, more commonly known as "The Drunk Tank." Every man arrested and brought to the Knox County Jail was placed there first. It was also the temporary holding cell for those of us who had been sentenced. This was during a time of heavy overcrowding in Tennessee's Correction Department. I was in disbelief as the guards placed me in a cell the size of a large bedroom packed end to end with all types of nervous convicts. The smell of musty body odor was breathtaking in a bad way. *Am I dreaming?* I kept pinching myself in hopes to wake up, but this was no dream.

There was a law that no prisoner was to be in "The

Drunk Tank" more than a few days. This gave me a little hope as I slept each night in irritating discomfort on the cold, rough, concrete floor. The few mats provided were already taken. Prisoners were being brought in and taken out at all hours, many of them were drunk or on drugs. An uncontrollable addict drugged out on PCP, commonly known as angel dust, was placed into the cell late one night while most were asleep. The hallucinations from the drug caused him to mistake me for the commode. As I pushed him away he released his urine on another unsuspecting inmate. Chaos broke out inside the jail as men fought like a pack of animals.

I hoped and prayed, *"Please let this all be a terrible nightmare that I will soon wake up out of."* The reality of existing in a world so inhumane was nearly unbearable. Just last week, I was destined to begin a beautiful journey of engineering success, living a life of luxury. I thought back on my childhood Bible Sunday school lessons. *Could this be how Joseph from the Bible felt?* I realized how much of a fool I was for forfeiting my dreams. A small ray of hope came when an inmate told me about the violent offender and the nonviolent offender cellblocks. The nonviolent offender cellblock would be very safe. The violent offender cellblock contained men who committed murder, manslaughter, aggravated assault, rape, armed robbery, and other hideous crimes. My only consolation was that I was a nonviolent offender and would eventually be safe with the others like me. Finally after thirty long days in, "The Drunk Tank," the guards came to take me to a cellblock. *Where are they taking me?*, I wondered. I had a sense of relief, knowing that wherever it was I would have a mattress instead of a concrete floor.

Wolf or Sheep!

The county jail guards were not shy about their abilities to control inmates. They never traveled alone with a prisoner. Most of them were rather large and had the ability to use their batons as a team to inflict severe pain and at times causing broken bones or concussions. Any appearance of an escape attempt or revolt could bring immediate wrath upon you. My mind had to quickly adjust to the reality that mercy often was not a right. It had to be earned in this place. This understanding could help me keep my body safe from the fury of the guards.

The guards opened the door to the cellblock. I walked down a pathway past some jail cells that contained up to two men each. I never made eye contact with any of the men that I passed by. My cell was the only one open. My roommate was a 5 foot 11 inch, slightly overweight African American male. First impressions can be deceptive in jail, as it is not full of honest upstanding citizens. Nevertheless, my roommate wanted peace as much as me. After all, I figured he too was happy to be out of "The Drunk Tank" and into the nonviolent offender cellblock.

I was in absolute dismay when my roommate told me his criminal charge was armed robbery! As he explained his lack of guilt, like most convicts, the fact that I had somehow been placed in the violent offender cellblock left me speechless. *This MUST be a mistake! What were the guards thinking? Did release from the "Drunk Tank" lead to a sentence of being beaten down by inmate terrorists?* Nobody but me was even concerned about why I was in the wrong cellblock. I felt so alone and without support.

There was no way in "hack" I could let anyone in this department know that I had committed a nansy-pansy little crime of hacking into a bank. As a matter of fact, it wouldn't be wise to mention the ability to hack into a bank around professional armed robbers. Suddenly, the loud noise of cells opening rang in my ears. It was time for lunch, which was held in the dayroom (like a cafeteria) with all the men in the cellblock. I saw tattoos, tops of jail suits around waists, cigarettes spouting heavy smoke, and a line of the city's most unwanted outlaws and thugs.

Everyone took a seat. The chairs and tables were cemented into the floor. We walked up to a hole in the bars to get our platter of lunch. I couldn't help but notice an average sized white man with a splint on his ring finger. My curiosity peaked when I saw another white man across the room with a splint on his ring finger also. A teenage boy came to sit with me. He was frantic to borrow some cigarettes. I didn't smoke. The boy was only seventeen years old. He became almost hysterical, breathing rapidly with a look of nervous, fright on his face. He was obviously trying to escape confrontation with someone, suspecting that he would come to the cellblock after him.

A few minutes later I heard a loud voice as the guards opened the door to the cellblock. A six-foot black male, fairly strong build, around thirty-eight years old with short uncombed hair entered the dayroom. He was obviously an egotistical tyrant who sought to rule the cellblock. Once he entered, he stopped at a table and yelled out "Wolf or Sheep?!" The men at the table yelled out, "Wolf!" He went table by table doing this. When he came to our table, the boy yelled out "Sheep!" The tyrant went off on the boy not having his cigarettes. The boy began to beg him not to break his finger. I was astonished at the boy's request. The tyrant explained, "I thought we had an agreement. An agreement is like a happy marriage. A ring is the symbol of that happy marriage. When a marriage is broken you take away the ring. Since the state don't let us have rings, I have to take the finger."

Without mercy, he tells his two thug friends to break the boy's finger. They grab him to break his finger. This was much too sadistic for my mind to conceive. *Was this really happening?* I couldn't believe what I was seeing. *Should I mind my own business and let the boy be tormented? Should I help the boy and risk my own life?* Time seemed to stand still for a moment, yet it didn't. The old Samurai Joe began to come alive again. *No! I would not let the boy be tortured without a fight.*

I quickly surveyed the room and saw the trays of food on the tables. I heard the guards down the walkway a bit. I now had a ridiculous plan that may save the boy and me. I knew that I would have to fight the tyrant for at least a short while. I saw a way to use time to my advantage in a rescue plan. *That's it! Here goes...*

Suddenly, I yelled out *"Sheep!"* The tyrant responded, "What did you say?!" I then spoke in a challenging way with absolutely no fear, *"I said Sheep!"* The tyrant was initially impressed, stating, "Finally, someone knows at their first meeting with me whether they were a wolf or a sheep." I then informed the tyrant of a little misunderstanding. I told him I was actually calling him a sheep. Intense anger bubbled up quickly in the tyrant as he promised to "bust me up." It was necessary to use my drama skills, so I made myself look totally out of my mind with my whole facial expression and body language. I wanted everyone to think I was completely out of my mind and deranged! I began to loudly "talk junk" right back at him and even threw the boy's platter of food into the jail bars. Food flew through the bars into the guard's walkway.

Getting the attention of the guards was my plan all along. I knew in a short time they would come running to check out what was going on. If I had to fight, I had hoped that the guards could possibly get there before I was maimed or killed. And oh, I *did* have to fight! Anticipating that the tyrant would soon swing at me, I had my hands on my platter to block it. He swung and hit the wide platter, and I lunged at him surprising the whole cellblock of inmates. My hands were very strong from years of push-ups on my fingertips. As the guards were running in, I clawed the tyrant's face leaving a long nasty scratch.

When the guards got close, I jumped away from the tyrant

and lay on the floor in total submission. Meanwhile, another guard took the maniacal tyrant away while he was yelling and screaming threats to kill me. All of this happened so fast; I impressed myself with my quick-wittedness. But my heart was now pounding with the expectation of being beaten by the guard's hard baton. Knowing the helpless boy was saved somehow gave me enough strength to take the beating like a man. As one guard simply touched me I jumped anticipating deep pain from the baton. The guards lightly laughed and left the cellblock. The tyrant was placed in a different violent offender cellblock. The inmates were happy he was gone. After the whole situation, the inmates must have thought I was truly insane, but my newfound respect was very welcoming. A familiar feeling came over me as I realized I was still Samurai Joe inside. The good guys weren't mistreated this time. The hero had prevailed. The victims were saved. Defense came to the rescue. Justice was served. I felt my integrity slowly being redeemed.

The reason for being placed in the violent offender cellblock was still unanswered. It was years after my incarceration that I found that my arrest record had stated that I "beat an officer" escaping from UTK security. Unfortunately, when I was originally arrested, I did resist arrest in a moment of confusion by jerking away in a self-defense move and hitting the UTK security officers arm to get free. Physically resisting arrest was probably more than enough for me to be considered a potential threat to inmates with nonviolent offences. My little skirmish with the tyrant did little to help my case to move to the nonviolent side of this metalhood either.

Within one week of being in the violent cellblock, a short white man in the guard's hallway walked right up to the bars of the dayroom carrying a Bible in his hand. He was the jail chaplain. He invited me to come to a worship service for the inmates. So on Sunday morning, I attended the service. I was pleasantly surprised when I saw people in street clothes sharing the gospel of Christ in the middle of the jail. Amazingly, convicts openly gave their lives to Christ right there on the spot. For the first time in years, I felt hope as I saw Jesus show His love through these faithful ambassadors, who took time from their lives to esteem men considered societies lowest. I took every opportunity to attend services.

The church services taught me the true difference between a wolf and a sheep. The tyrant was a wolf who sought to bring havoc against righteous attitudes like love, peace, and joy. In my heart I wanted to learn more about the "sheep", those who showed humility and concern for others like the jail chaplain, because it seemed that they carried some type of hidden power to overcome adversity. At least now, I was beginning to see my plea for help being answered as peace started to settle in my soul. Soon, I was to learn that sometimes God answers prayer in the most unexpected places.

Chapter 5

THE FIGHT OF MY LIFE

I had now been in jail for over seven months, and by the grace of God I had been spared from further dangerous brawls in the violent offender cellblock.

During this time I had only told a few of my friends and family that I was incarcerated. My decision to isolate myself from them left me with little support from the outside. I felt far too much shame to have my friends publicize my whereabouts. The weekly church service became my primary source of encouragement. Though still immature in my faith, I had enough knowledge to realize that there was hope for a brighter future. All I had to do now was what Grandmama always told me; trust God in all things, yet somehow that always seemed easier to say than do.

Country Music Salvation

After spending months in the Knoxville county jails, guards unexpectedly arrived one morning, and took me; hands and feet clad in shackles to another jail in upper East Tennessee on a bus full of mostly white inmates. There was one young black guy on the bus, whom I had not previously met, who continually bragged about himself. Entering the cellblock for the first time, we could see that it opened into a dayroom. A semi-circle of jail cells along the wall surrounded the dayroom. There were also lunch tables cemented to the floor in the center of the room. Country music happened to be playing loudly on a little stereo sitting on one of the tables in the middle of the dayroom. The doors of the cells were closed and no one was in sight. The young black guy was greatly annoyed by the country music and openly showed his disgust by turning off the stereo. A white man yelled from inside the cells, "Turn the music back on." The young black guy shouted obscenities at the yeller and loudly criticized the country music. I thought, *"Oh my goodness. What is this boy doing? Is he trying to get killed our first day here?"*

Suddenly, the sounds of fists against hands began to break out in one cell. The next cell joined in, and then the next until the sound of fists against hands were heard throughout all the cells. Tension filled the air. To my horror, a loud buzz, then the click of the cell doors unlocking filled the room. Gradually, the doors of the cellblock opened simultaneously. If there had ever been a time in my life in which I was afraid of anything, it would be what I encountered next. Dozens of tattooed, t-shirt wearing white men came walking out of their cells beating their fists in their hands. I had never used the term redneck in describing a white man, but if I were to do so, this little army of angry, country music loving inmates would have fit that description perfectly.

It was close to chow time, and I could tell that these men wanted charbroiled black steak as the main course, and our hides would provide the fresh meat. Begging for mercy would have just fed their thirst for blood. My breath almost left me as I anticipated an imminent gang beating. In a desperate thought, I turned to yell for the guard, but I didn't have to; he was at the door watching all along, smiling with satisfaction. *What? But how could he...? Why wasn't he...?*

Then this large, "cornbread fed" white man who must have been the leader came walking out of his cell. Tattoos of skulls and spiders were scattered all over his body. His sleeves were torn on both arms as if he were always hot.

His head was shaved and marked from several razor cuts. I instantly knew that this man just loved himself some country music. Now it had been turned off, and he was mad! I realized that this man could easily kill me had the others held me while he beat me.

I thought, *"OH MY GOD! Were you teasing me with your love through the church people in the last jail? Were they sent to the jail to prepare me to soon meet my Maker? Please Jesus, I need the answer to one question. Did You by chance follow me here? If so, please...please...please... if you don't mind, I need You to prove that You are here, and could You do it really fast?"*

As the white, hillbilly, human demolition leader slowly walked toward the young black guy and me, suddenly I had the most creative thought, *TURN THE COUNTRY MUSIC BACK ON AND SING!* When we first arrived, the stereo was playing an old country classic, one of my favorite albums growing up (Remember, "I was country when country wasn't cool.") I turned the song back on and screamed, "YEEEEE HAAAA!!" and sang melodiously with the country music. I even did a little jig with it. The white leader coming to annihilate us stopped in his tracks, not knowing what to think at first. He was so disarmed that he began to laugh uncontrollably. Then the whole cellblock of white inmates also began laughing as I kept on singing.

After the song was over, I apologized for the young black guy's ignorance in criticizing such music. We were forgiven. *Whew, Thank you God!* I was ecstatic, but remained cool. That moment was one of the greatest reliefs in my life. Without question, only God could have saved me from such an impossible situation. It was then that I unknowingly started to realize how much of a Father, God was to me. He supported and protected me more than Samurai Joe ever could. Imagine that.

Computer Trustee

After a few days, the sheriff had a guard take me out of the cellblock and bring me to his office. The jail had a new computer system issued by the Corrections Department and nobody on staff knew how to use it. He didn't have funds in his budget to hire a computer expert, so he was searching to see if an inmate could help his staff learn the new computer system. I had plenty of competition in computer skills in the outside world, but in jail, there was no one that could possibly out "geek" me. Thankfully, they became acquainted with me and soon offered to make me a trustee, someone who receives special rights and privileges in exchange for their services or jobs they are responsible for within a jail/prison.

I gratefully accepted the position! It was almost too good to be true. Ironically, as I look back on this, I can see how God was using the very gift I abused in college to help others in prison; He was exalting me. Immediately, I was moved out of the general cellblock to the trustee quarters, which seemed like a real apartment. My duties included teaching the staff how to use their new computers and giving myself and other inmates time or other credits for good behavior. As a result of these particular credits an inmate could be released from jail weeks earlier.

Much to my delight, Christian counselors came to visit the jail. They suggested a great idea; that I serve as the teacher over a tutorial class, to which the sheriff agreed, trusting me to help approximately thirty inmates secure their GED. It was a time of honor for me in which I felt the integrity of my character being restored. It gave me a sense of worth and value again. It was nice feeling trusted. I felt a part of Samurai Joe being revived once again, only in a peaceable way. *Could this have something to do with God?* I wondered. Life had become somewhat of a joy for me in this unlikely place, as I realized God was allowing things to go well for me.

Jesus was obviously keeping the perks coming. Quickly,

I became the most popular inmate in jail. I had the trust of the sheriff to go outside on the front patio at anytime. I was also given the indulgence to work out in the weight room frequently, and freedom to go to the cafeteria. Over several months of eating a heavy protein diet and lifting weights, I went from 154 pounds to 165 pounds of hard body weight.

My reward for teaching my white inmate friends came one day as one of them was being released. He asked me to meet his son. My friend's son said, "You're the one who helped my daddy finish high school." The little boy then gave me a big hug. I felt honored to have warranted such appreciation. His innocence reminded me of someone I used to know...me. How far had I strayed away from myself?

A few days later, a former college female friend, who treated me as a brother, came to visit. When she hugged me, I couldn't let her go. I had kept the tears pent up inside me, since the first day of jail. In the former jail in Knoxville, my punishment included not being able to receive visitors from any friends or family outside of talking through a glass booth. Now miles from the Knoxville jail, I was allowed a hug from a friend. I cried silently with tears flowing like a river. I had forgotten what a simple embrace of love felt like. The simple things of life are often taken for granted until they are taken away.

A few weeks later it was a unanimous decision from the sheriff and the Christian counselors to help me obtain Work Release to complete the little work left on my engineering degree. They wanted to repay me in some way for aiding the inmates and the staff. A state senator was contacted and agreed to work out a plan that would grant me Work Release. I was completely elated, until I was told that there was a stipulation. Up until this point, I had only been in the jail system. Work Release required being classified into the prison system. This meant I would have to relocate to Brushy Mountain State Penitentiary, the most notorious prison in Tennessee, filled with the state's most hardened criminals.

Due to the overcrowded situation in Tennessee, the only men sent to Brushy Mountain at the time were extremely violent offenders who had a minimum of ten years of time to serve. Most prisoners there had over twenty years and many had life sentences. I was at a crossroads of making a very important decision: 1) I could opt to stay at the jail in what was considered luxury as an inmate and pass up the opportunity to complete my final two college courses while serving my time or 2) I could go through Brushy Mountain for only six days and be allowed Work Release to obtain the degree I had worked so hard at earning. I so desperately wanted to return to the outside world and taste the pleasures of freedom once again, even if it was only for a few hours a week. But, was it worth serving six days in a notorious prison?

> *I can do this. Look at all I have endured. Surely it won't be that bad. I can handle anything, now. I'm even physically stronger and fit. All I have to do is stay in my cell the whole time and never go out for recreation with other inmates. Of course, that's it!*

I agreed to leave my life of inmate-lushness and do whatever it took to go after the degree that slipped through my hands.

Fight or Die

The assistant sheriff and I arrived at Brushy Mountain. I gasped when my eyes focused on the prison. This prison was built on the backside of a mountain and had the appearance of a haunted castle. After coming through the tall metal doors, I was handed over to the Brushy Mountain prison guard. They immediately slapped on the handcuffs. I said "bye" to my

assistant sheriff friend. As I walked, my senses started to kick
in as I noticed the discord and felt the intense danger of this
place through the attitudes of the inmates and guards. I could
feel excessive hatred and anger; such gloom, heaviness and
an eerie tension consumed the atmosphere. I had the feeling
that I had made a terrible life-threatening mistake.

My first experience in the cafeteria was horrific. I watched
as an inmate got his ear cut off by a rival. After all the commotion, I sat down with a white man in the cafeteria to eat
lunch. He had been transferred to Brushy the same day. We
saw each other in the intake office. I was suddenly alarmed
when I looked at him and noticed his eyes were staring in
a daze focused on someone behind me while at the same
time I felt hot air breathing down upon me. The man behind
me pulled out a homemade knife called a shank, showed it
to him and threatened, "If you don't get up right now, I'm
going to shank him in the back." He was referring to me. The
prison was mostly racially segregated. My friend at the table
resisted changing seats at first, but he was only putting me
in danger. I managed to convince him to move by raising my
eyebrows and nodding my head communicating to him he
needed to move. I was extremely aware of the ludicrous state
of this man holding a weapon in his hand. I began to wonder
just how deep a mistake I had made in leaving my inmate
paradise. Nevertheless, I held to my original convictions.

The recreation area of Brushy Mountain was the most
dangerous place. For five days the cell doors opened for recreation, and each day I stayed in my cell. On the sixth day,
to my surprise a familiar face walked up to my cell. It was
a friend from the Knoxville county jail. He had become a
trustee in this prison and was cleaning the walkway by my
cell. He convinced me that it was safe to come to the gym for
recreation for just one day. So when the guards opened the
cells, I went to the gym.

Suddenly, a perplexing commotion was brewing. Some

of the inmates bolted out of the gym, while the remaining few of them began to open their uniforms and tie them off just above their waist exposing their chests. I knew that this was a ritual before a fight, so I attempted to slip out, but the inmates formed a circle around me preventing me from leaving. No one said a word. I could feel my head getting warm in anticipation of danger. The stage was set for an action-packed scene, and apparently, I was a principle character. With increasing heaviness, the footsteps of a single man could be heard walking toward the small circle of men. I could tell that the man was big. The circle opened to let him in. The first thing I noticed upon looking at the man was a long ugly facial scar.

I stood there in utter shock. The man was the tyrant I briefly fought in the Knoxville jail, and he and other violent offenders had been sent to Brushy Mountain months before I arrived. *How could this be happening to me?* It didn't take much to realize my friend had been threatened to lure me to the gym or else jeopardize his own life and safety. Initially, I felt tricked and betrayed until I quickly realized that the young man was trying to live; not die. This war game consisted of fighting one man from the circle. If I won, then I would fight another, until eventual defeat. The unspoken law of jail was to beat a person within an inch of their life to earn respect. The unspoken law of prison was...well...there were no laws. Due to my new size and strength from working out, I confidently and foolishly had no fear and welcomed a few good one on one fights, knowing I was more than capable to take some bullies out!

The judgment pronounced openly by the tyrant was extremely graphic and made known to everyone who had ears to hear. If I lost to one man, both my friend and I would be tortured first by having all our fingers broken, and then beaten without mercy by having our ribs broken to a point that the damage would cause our lungs to collapse. It was evident, the tyrant's rage and desire for revenge was so tremendous that he refused to let me come out alive.

I could not hold back my emotions. Anger quickly rose in me, and I decided that enough was enough. Now, very fit and strong from months of exercise along with martial arts training, I refused to go down. Surrounded by attackers, I began to feel empowered to fight. I wanted to defeat them all! Fear was no longer an option. In fact, it did not exist in these moments. I had now fully transformed. I was a Samurai again.

The first guy came at me and received an unexpected quick beat down. After this turn of events, the others were reluctant to face me, so I quickly pushed through the circle and ran outside the gym. The tyrant and maybe some of the others had a shank. Taking my trustee friend with me, I had to find a place more suitable for fighting. As a janitorial trustee, my friend could not open jail cells but did have access to some of the prison's rooms and offices. I was looking for a room to escape and maybe find objects that could be used as weapons. Like all inmates up to no good, our assailants wanted to avoid the attention of the guards and suddenly stopped running after us. On the inside, I wanted to stop and fight, but on the outside, I had to instinctively get away. Without many routes of escape we were quickly found by one of our attackers. Feeling somewhat responsible for the trustee, I protected him by taking down the attacker without much effort. Then the tyrant arrived.

I rushed him like a freight train. He swung at me with the shank and, I somehow caused him to drop it. All the anger of being sent to jail, all the resentment of leaving my dream life, all the fury of being forced to fight, all the rage of being thrown in an inescapable war game, and every ounce of madness inside me was unleashed on my enemy. His cohorts and other inmates stared in dismay as they saw me beat him down. They did nothing but watched. I beat him so bad, he lay on the ground motionless.

Then the guards came running. As I was being taken away, in the distance I could hear, "I can't feel a pulse, hurry."

Forty Days in the Hole

The guards placed me in solitary confinement for forty days at the warden's request. A man can go crazy alone in a wet, cold room with no daylight, clock, television, radio, or contact with anyone. At the mercy of the guards, in my mind even the safety of my food was suspect. Living constantly in the unknown, I didn't know what depths of torment awaited me.

Agonizing thoughts filled my mind as the very torment I fought all of my life was staring me right in the face, and I couldn't run from it: ABANDONMENT! Unfortunately for me, I couldn't fight this bully called abandonment, nor could I beat it down physically. It was too strong. I felt that I was losing the battle:

> *It is true. I am really all alone now, a reality to which I cannot deny. I'm buried alive underground in this hole. Nobody I care about even knows. Do they even care? My dad would surely never come to this place to see me, but something deep down inside my soul wants him to so badly. Nobody cares! I'm losing my mind. I won't eat. What if the food's poisoned? I'm so hungry!*

Days and nights were one and the same. I tried to conjure up a fantasy realm and place my mind in another reality time after time, yet it didn't work. Not even my imagination could help me escape this place. *Where am I? God, are you there? Jesus, are you with me?* Oh, those were dark times. I was starving for numerous things...so many. I longed for a touch, a voice, a hug...SOMETHING assuring me I was loved and not forgotten. So much bitterness was pinned up inside that ate away my very sanity. Waking up in cold sweats and horror, the nightmares alone were a living torture as I sorrowfully wondered if I had killed the tyrant.

Gratefully, I was allowed to get a letter from my family. In great anticipation, I moved as close as I could to a dim light shining into the room, yet still had to strain to read it. I had hoped that it would bring me hope and happiness, yet it only heightened my misery when I learned that my grandmother had colon cancer, and was given only a few months to live. This was devastating news to me. It was almost unbearable. *How much more can I take? GOD! ARE YOU THERE? PLEASE rescue me.* I was at the point of no return mentally, blaming myself for so much pain.

I fell asleep one night, or was it one day? Either way, I had a dream of a red rose floating down a peaceful river. *What did this mean?* My only thought was the memory of husbands giving their wives a red rose as a symbol of love. Maybe, just maybe, God was telling me that He still loved me regardless of all my wrong decisions and sins. Maybe by some long shot it was a foreshadowing of a divinely chosen young lady who would be endowed with a love for me that would prove to be unconditional. Whatever the message was, I had reached the place of feeling like a nothing.

Released from Prison

After solitary confinement, I was sent immediately to Work Release in Knoxville for a few months, but I lost my opportunity to go to UT and finish the final class. I wasn't even allowed to tutor other inmates or leave on a work assignment picking up trash. The violent battle at Brushy Mountain caused me to only qualify as a janitor for those final few months of incarceration with almost no privileges.

After eighteen months of an unforgettable jail and prison nightmare, I was released to a halfway house in Knoxville close to UTK. I completed one of the two classes needed for graduation, but I was kicked out of the halfway house for failure to find a job. I was forced to live without a home in a small borrowed car. At times I was able to sleep on couches in the apartment of a couple of merciful fraternity brothers. I never would have thought I would be so displaced and homeless. Unable to function in Knoxville anymore, let alone complete my final engineering class, I got a parole transfer to move to Nashville, hoping to escape my past and start some type of life.

Just a few weeks after arriving in Nashville, my grandmother died in my mother's arms at my childhood home, just 65 miles away from me. With my greatest life coach now gone, I thought that maybe I could complete the final engineering class by correspondence. This plan seemed useless, because I was marked with the stigma of being an ex-convict, and carried a violent prison record. *Who would hire me now?*

Does God somehow use nobodies? I hoped so, because it was now my only qualification...

Chapter 6

HER LOVE CHANGED MY WORLD

When anyone asked me the true reason for moving to Nashville, in 1990 at age 28, I could give no logical response. Truth is, I didn't have anywhere else to go. One reason was to be closer to visit my grandmother in her last days alive on earth. In reality, an undefined compulsion drove me to move there. Like a master guiding a lost wartorn horse with a whistle, God led me to the city that held the answers to my destiny.

Dodging My Record to Make a Living

A fraternity brother, who no longer lived in Nashville, got his mother's permission to allow me to temporarily live in his basement bedroom in her house. The mother lived alone in the upper level and welcomed my being there to keep watch over the house. My rent was very low, but not free. Unfortunately even for a poor ex-convict, buying food was a necessity. I had to earn a living somehow.

I got an intriguing idea that could only be attributed to God granting wisdom. Since I needed employment, but wanted to avoid a repeat of a brief Knoxville post-prison job that ended in disaster, my natural thoughts gravitated to using my dormant talents. I began to ponder what talents I possessed from previous work experiences that would not require a background check. I knew that I would be unable to land a high paying single job anymore, so I had to think outside of the box. An idea came to mind of taking my versatile skills of music, computer and physical strength and somehow combining these skills in part-time and freelance work.

In the African American church, talented musicians are often paid. I began playing saxophone for my church choir in the eighth grade. Throughout college I played for a popular university gospel choir. With a church on nearly every corner, I felt Nashville was a prime location to freelance as a musician. Even better, sweet sounding saxophone players were rare in many Nashville churches and greatly sought after during this time. That was the reality, but I did not yet emotionally have the motivation to sell my abilities. I can recall the way I felt like it was yesterday.

How could I feel worthy of compensation from a church? I literally don't feel worth two cents. I won't be able to find a job. Nobody wants to hire a convicted criminal, especially, not a violent offender. I can't even get a regular job. What would a church think of me? Why would they want to hire a former convict? It's no use. *They don't want me. What am I going to do now? How could this be happening to me? I really feel ludicrous now, in a world unknown to me. I could adapt so well all my life. Why is this such a challenge for me?*

I thought once I was released from prison I would be free, only to find myself in larger shackles within my mind. Anguish and distress haunted me every time I would meet someone new. I wouldn't dare befriend someone or get close to them, fearing that they would hate and reject me. Trapped in a circuit with a familiar enemy, abandonment, my emotions were battered all over again.

Since there was so much mental anguish, I decided to stay to myself so nobody could hurt me, and I wouldn't scare them off. I had come to accept that I had come out of prison marked for life with a terrible past that needed to be kept hidden. I was on edge with people finding out about my past of incarceration. The fear of rejection was again showing up in my life everyday.

Despite all the mental confusion about my self worth, I cranked up enough courage to seek temporary employment for a church as a musician: saxophonist. I hadn't learned that I should view it as serving God just yet. I just needed some MONEY! Somehow, I got connected with a medium-sized church, and began earning a little money.

Another creative thought came in my mind one Sunday while playing for a choir. Practically, every African American church in the country purchased some type of bulletin cover from a Christian supply store to copy information for their Sunday morning order of service. I thought that with a little computer savvy, I could begin using copyright-free clip-art packages to create my own bulletin covers at a lower cost for the churches. I felt that in a few short months, several churches would take the bait, and I would then have a thriving business designing and typesetting bulletins. Even though the concept was great, it too came with the emotional turmoil of self-unworthiness.

While looking in "Want Ads" one day in September, I saw an ad for a temporary company, and decided that I would give that a try before presenting the bulletin idea to churches. Of course, the one great stipulation would be getting around the background check radar, because again, the change from all American boy to ex-convict left a fear of feeling ashamed for anyone to know my past. Nevertheless, I felt that I had no choice. Nobody was going to financially support a well and able-bodied man. I went to the temporary company and applied. The manager was so focused on my computer experience at Eastman Kodak that she never noticed that I didn't check the prior felony question. Though feeling somewhat guilty, I didn't bring it to her attention.

The manager was so impressed by my skills that she called me back that day before leaving her office. I had my first temporary job! The contract was in a department with the State of Tennessee. The drastic difference in pay from my former engineering cooperative job to a temporary job was challenging, but I knew "beggars can't be choosers." I would have taken the job for pennies had I known what God had set up to happen next.

She Walked Into My Life

The prison experience opened my heart to begin listening to God, but I needed someone to help me walk this out. With no one in my daily life for encouragement, the isolation of loneliness was my only companion. So it continued; the fear of people rejecting me fueled my segregation from others. Hopefully, God would use this new job to bring a ray of light in my life. After all, I was beginning a new chapter in my life having turned 29 years old the month prior.

On the first morning of my job, I sat on a chair inside an office cubicle waiting for my boss. I was feeling safe hidden from the site of others in the room. It was slightly startling when a beautiful young lady walked inside the cubicle right in front of me. If a black man can blush, I did. She was obviously much younger than me, but she had this interesting mature composure. When she turned her head, I fought hard to not scan her body shape, but it was to no avail. My thoughts were, "Ok, get a grip on yourself and come to your senses. She's much too young for you. Besides, remember that she would never find you worthy anyway."

We began to exchange questions? She was taking her first semester break from college to earn some money. She had been sent to the same temporary position a few days before me. When I was questioned, to avoid being totally deceptive, I told her that I had been "locked away for a while winning a few personal battles." After the boss came and gave our duties, we literally worked hand in hand separating papers and stuffing envelopes. She had a welcomed peaceful disposition; an air of humility unlike any of her female peers. She was delightful to work with. She was smart. She was funny. She was Denise.

After the first day of work, silly thoughts entered my mind. Based on my experiences with college girlfriends, I assumed that all beautiful young ladies had to be won over with money, charm, or stunning good looks. Well, I didn't possess any of those. Then I thought that she would probably want a man that was tall, dark, and handsome. My semi-sweet chocolate complexion provided me with at least one of these. Hope was alive! But I was not seeking a relationship with *any* woman, especially one of her class. It was way too risky considering my decision to open up to no one. Nightmares of prison battles and the fear of new acquaintances discovering my shameful past kept me from considering her a viable candidate for marriage. And oh yea, she was *still* too young for me. Honestly, I could make no sense of how I felt inside, as I now found myself confused about life and it's inevitable adventures.

A Divine Plan of Romance

Initially, neither one of us knew that we had been placed in a strategic plan for God to someday unite us in marriage. First, I believe the Lord provided an inescapable way for Denise and I to spend lots of time together. She lived five minutes from my neighborhood and she did not have a car, so she accepted a ride with me to and from work each day. This meant from 7:30 am to 5:00 pm we were constantly together. We quickly became very close friends. She was unbelievably easy to converse with, and at times I had to ask her if she was real. Friendship would be the first key to our unbreakable love affair.

Second, I believe the Lord provided a hidden way for us

to grow emotionally intimate before we knew it was happening. Oh yes, did I mention that Denise had a boyfriend, whom her family loved and expected her to marry someday. He was a tall attractive football player and long time family friend who had been attending college with her, but they were having major emotional problems. Her boyfriend often incited her to anger, simply because he thought she was, "so cute when she was mad," however she expressed to me her distaste of his eerie pursuit of discord. During my college days, I had experienced a measure of success with the ladies, so I extended my services free of charge as a relationship counselor. Let's just say she found my relational advice quite intriguing. Regardless whether she or I initiated the conversation, each time she needed relationship counsel, we learned more about each other's passion and similar definition of true love.

One day while on lunch break, I asked her a question: "What type of man would you like to marry someday?" Her answer was, "A man like you." With that answer the little relationship hints that were exchanged between us grew substantially. I could not believe this was happening to me. *Me? Am I dreaming? What did she see? What kind of woman was she to look at me with desire? God, have you really looked down and smiled on me?* My life had clearly made a total change for the better. Whatever was happening I didn't want it to stop! I couldn't believe all this was for me!

About two months after we met, I took her on a friendly date to Red Lobster for her twentieth birthday. The nine-year difference in our age was somewhat of a roadblock in my mind, but I did manage to find some contentment with it. As for me, the perception of being young nine years longer made me feel much better than being nine years older. But she didn't care about this at all- no, not one bit...and do you want to know why? Well, I'll tell you. I had not told her my age yet. I couldn't risk the dream ending this soon. Besides, she still had that boyfriend hanging out on the sidelines. I couldn't allow myself to be too hopeful. She walked out to my car dressed in a short silky black dress. She placed something in the trunk of my car and got in. I must confess. That night I wanted her for dinner.

We had a wonderful dinner at Red Lobster. After enjoying the last bite, Denise giddily excused herself from the table and went to the trunk of the car to reveal her surprise for me. Unexpectedly, she walked back inside Red Lobster carrying cookies on an old crusty burnt color-worn pan that looked like her grandmother had used as a child. The employees only watched, as she was totally innocent and free from embarrassment in breaking the protocol of a nice restaurant. I, on the other hand, wanted to crawl slowly under the table and hide, as we became the comical center of attention for the night. Nevertheless, her motive of giving and lack of concern for others' adverse opinion was precious to me.

She later let me know that she had never before cooked anything for a male friend and reluctantly questioned her own actions. It was a rather bold act of kindness that could have been easily taken as a flirtatious gesture. Amazingly, when I took her back home, our lips softly touched as we kissed each other goodnight. This first kiss set me ablaze, and it was as if fireworks had gone off and lit up the dark sky! As I walked away from this intimate moment, an unfamiliar, warm sensation, stirred within my heart and it felt as if I was still in a beautiful dream of the night. *Could there be a slight chance of a future with her? Am I good enough for her to love?* It had happened so stealthily, I was unaware how deeply I had already fallen for her. What a huge risk I was taking!

Love Overlooks My Past

A few weeks following her birthday, I could not deny my curiosity about Denise and whether if she by some chance

79

could be a potential companion for me. This seemed ludicrous to me because of the age difference. Without knowing my age, Denise's family also believed that I was too old for her. One evening while visiting her family, they asked of my age. Denise also wanted to know my age, but for a motive of determining more on our compatibility. I wouldn't disclose it, which seemed fairly rude to everyone. They each had a partial frown on their face. They did not let the question go.

In the opinion of Denise's parents, age difference was a big strike against our relationship. They also did not want her to give up on her other boyfriend, whom they knew well and admired. They began a guessing game to discover my age. One of them guessed twenty-six and believed it. I unwisely let them believe what they wanted. It didn't matter to me. I convinced myself to believe that no woman, young or old, would desire me once they learned of the criminal and violent events in my background. It would all be over anyway with the blink of an eye. I was no longer the optimistic all American boy who had everything under control according to strategic planning.

I never expected my relationship with Denise to blossom as it did. The vast amount of our quality time together contrasted with the frequent fights with her boyfriend and caused their relationship to slip quickly away. I watched nervously each day, as this attractive young lady sought to know me more. I thought, "Oh Lord, please don't let me lose her friendship, and how can I tell her who I am?" I was so afraid of things going wrong that would persuade her to leave me. So my hidden secret was always hanging over me threatening to destroy what I had always longed for in a true friend. A taunting thought would continually plague me: *How long would it be before she found out?*

Then one day while eating lunch, she pulled out of her purse a letter for me written on paper designed for a mainframe computer printer. The use of this type of paper was in the process of becoming obsolete. Initially, I was afraid that somehow she had discovered my recent tragic past, which would result in losing her wonderful friendship. *Did she now know of the computer hacking incident? Was this a sarcastic punishment for hiding my past?* I could have not been more mistaken.

As she gave me the letter, it was obvious that she had written something that she was nervous in revealing. I noticed she was rubbing her hands together. Her chest was rising higher from taking deeper breathes of air in anticipation of my response. Within the letter she explained how much she cherished the joy of our companionship. Then she had written a statement that caused my hands to slightly shake from being stunned. She wrote that God had filled her heart with the knowledge that we would someday be married to each other.

(Drum roll..cymbal crash) What?!

Nothing in my life had prepared me for this bold, yet humble remark. I kept holding the paper pretending to be a slow reader hoping that she would get her focus off my facial response. I fought hard to conceal the degree that this letter was totally bushwhacking my heart. All I could do was softly say to her, "Wow!", and then say "Wow!" again. My lack of words and inability to stop moving in my seat must have led her to assure me that it was far from her character to make a prediction this bold, but she stuck with her belief. At that moment, thoughts of confusion concerning Denise filled my mind.

How could all this happen? Does she know I am beginning to desire her much more than a friend? Now she will really hate me when she learns who I am. My punishment will be never

*to see her again. My only friend will surely
leave me. ...or could Denise in some crazy
twist of life be the lovely rose God showed me
in the dream while in solitary confinement?*

The yearning to be open about my past grew substantially. Within days of receiving the letter we sat alone one evening. I placed myself in the position of vulnerability with Denise as I disclosed my destructive past. As tears began to roll down my face, I told her how pride in computer hacking deceived me, how far my fall had taken me, how dangerous prison had been, how challenging it was finding jobs as an ex-convict, how undesirable my position as a man had truly become.

As I turned my head from her, she placed her hand on my chin and turned it back holding me warmly in her arms. *How in the world did she know I so DESPERATELY needed to be embraced?* I wept in shame holding my head low. She guided my chin upward with her soft hands and whispered, "Chin up...listen to me. You are not the same person as you were then. You don't have to fight anymore. Let the past be just that...the past." *How did she KNOOOOWWW??? I don't want to fight anymore.* My emotions were released with a climatic sob and deep cry of remorse. I was so overwhelmed. So much had been pinned up inside all this time. She *had* to be my rose. She understood! I had wanted to be accepted and loved for so long, but I didn't think I ever could.

Is she in love with me?

Whether she was or not, her comforting embrace was evidence that she accepted me.

Chapter 7

BEAUTIFUL MUSIC TOGETHER

The dread that hovered over me was finally confronted and resolved. As I reflect on that night I lay vulnerably cuddled in her arms, there is yet something that still stirs my heart. A simple act of love never fails no matter what the circumstance. It had totally changed my whole world. A sigh of great relief had engulfed me, knowing that none of my words had caused Denise to judge me or diminished her belief in the future union that God had prepared for us. Later, she let me know what she saw in those intimate moments. She said that at my core, she saw a gentle, humble man of honor that was kind, considerate, and sincere, unlike any man she had ever met. Funny thing is, once I revealed the truth about my past she was even more certain and affirmed in her faith about what God had told her. Not many days after my confession, she broke up with her boyfriend. With this, we were both now free to become more acquainted with one another and begin our inescapable romance.

Perfect Harmony

My involvement with Denise often revolved around music from the first day we met. She would frequently invite me to her family's gospel group's rehearsal, deep in the boonies of a neighboring county, and I would respect-fully decline to attend. I was hesitant in attending, because I had imagined, a loud-singing, overall-wearing, turnip-green picking quartet who didn't know the difference between a piano and an organ. The clincher to her invitation was always the chance to hear her uncle play the electronic keyboard. At the time he allegedly had been the great Ray Charles' organ player for over two decades. That indeed fascinated me, yet I allowed my initial imaginings to get the better of me, at least for a while longer.

At a point, I took Denise to visit my residence, and she noticed my saxophone. She looked at me with curiosity, as if wondering if I actively played it. I would have loved to woo her with my styling, but I didn't like playing without accom-paniment from a pianist. I changed out of my office shirt into a tank top, while she stood in the hallway. I grasped this opportunity to show off my muscular physique. The urge to impress her overcame me. When I came out into the hallway I slightly held my chest and arms in a flex position to exag-gerate my muscle size and distinctiveness. She pretended not to notice me, though we both knew she did.

To divert the topic on both of our minds, Denise's next move greatly impressed me. She sat down at the piano and played a tune her mother had taught her. Now, there's a sound in music that enlightens the soul like the soothing crackle of fire burning hot coals in a fireplace on a cold winter's night. These types of music waves can be defined only by saying, "Oooooh, that's good." In her modesty, she would take no credit for having affected me that way.

Throughout my college years, I had openly shared with my friends the desire to marry a fellow musician who shared the same love for music. This was definitely a quality that was required, though she was clueless of my innermost dream of a companion. *Could this be another sign from God that what she said was true? Am I really her husband? She really is my wife, isn't she?* Denise's short melody on the piano was enough for me to finally accept her invitation to hear her family group.

A few days later we travelled to her family's gospel group's rehearsal. My mission was to examine the seemingly exaggerated claims of her family's musical abilities. We arrived slightly late. The group was comprised of nine to ten women, and Denise's uncle played electronic keyboard for them. Upon entering, I was surprised to see all kinds of musical instruments throughout the room. With all of the equipment, it looked like a "major heavy duty" music studio; mixing boards, microphone stands, and other musical equipment flanked the room. I sat down feeling so stupid for stereotyping her musical family.

Shortly after introductions, her uncle began to play. His fingers seemed to glide from one key to another flawlessly. There is a noticeable distinction between a "good" musician and a "great" one. This man was definitely a master keyboardist. Now, I had played with many great musicians, but rarely had I witnessed one with this man's abilities. My surprise escalated when her uncle was replaced on the keyboard in the middle of a song by her oldest aunt without a break in the flow of music or sweetness in sound. Later, I learned that the family group had several more experienced musicians.

The wonder of the night was not yet over. These extremely kind-hearted women could accomplish a feat rarely attempted in gospel music at the time: singing six-part harmony with extraordinary ease. Occasionally, Denise's eye would twinkle at me, while she sang. I was confounded with jaw-dropping adulation at what I was hearing. After the rehearsal, I had learned that each woman possessed the impeccable ability to create harmonies and that Denise had neglected to mention that her uncle had also played with B. B. King and other famous artists. Needless to say, that night had caught me completely off guard.

After seeing Denise's musical talent, I accepted an invitation from her to attend a concert in which several gospel choirs would minister. Her mother was the piano player for one of the choirs. As her mother sat down at the piano, Denise sat down at the drums. *What on earth is she doing sitting in the drummer's seat?* She hit four rim shots on the drums to start the song. Her mother took the cue, and started playing the piano as Denise carried the beat on the drums. The crowd clapped as this young lady's dynamic rhythm filled the church. I sat smiling with an even deeper appreciation for Denise, the musician. Seems I wasn't the only one gifted with versatility. What an incredible night!

As weeks progressed, worship leaders began to call me in quest of seeking a saxophonist to add flavor to their band and each performance would lead to the next as invitations kicked up. On several occasions, congregations were simply amazed, especially when my secret weapon, Denise, started playing the drums! This was the most fun I had experienced since my college years. What's more, we received compensation for it. Not even a year ago, I felt unworthy of playing at a church, and now, I was accepted and requested at multiple ones. At last, I had started to feel some security in whom I was becoming, knowing that my past really didn't matter.

During these specials times, Denise and I were getting closer and closer, seemingly inseparable to her family and friends, as we were almost always side-by-side. I never expected to have this deep of a desire to be with someone all the time. I literally woke up each day with the excitement of simply seeing her smile and feeling her compassionate hug. I couldn't wait to see her.

Deal or No Deal

On August 22, 1991, just less than a year after we first met, I turned thirty years old. Since my age had not come up again after the family interrogation, I still had not told

Denise my true age, which posed a dilemma. She was still under the persuasion that I was twenty-six. *How could I have allowed this to go one for so long? I should have told her long ago? Obviously, I was wrong about this not developing into a relationship. How could I have been so wrong?* My initial belief that Denise and I would in no way ever become a couple was terribly miscalculated. Obviously God had another viewpoint. Now was the time to be forthright with Denise. With her parents already seeking our demise, I knew that I was between a rock and a hard place on this issue, because I could not allow her to continue in deception. Much to my misfortune, a human can't have a birthday and stay the same age as the previous year, so I had to come clean on my actual age.

One night after a date, while sitting in the car I revealed my age to her. Her mouth flew open, and her eyes widened as she began shaking her head as if to say, *"No, you've got to be kidding me."* I could only imagine what she was thinking, and it was torture not to hear her speak. The disappointment on her face caused my heart to sink. I felt horrible for what she would have to bear when she told her family. After all, her family had guessed that I was only six years her elder. Her countenance quickly graduated to anger; not the kind of anger that says, "I'M ABOUT TO SLAP YOUR FACE OFF!" then followed by a make-up session. Quite the contrary, this was the kind of anger that says, "YOU JUST MESSED EVERYTHING UP!" I would have gladly taken a big slap instead.

The odds of a future relationship with Denise now seemed low. She had gotten out of my car and had not even turned back to wave to me. I felt like the king of monumental mistakes. To add to my hurt, Denise was no longer working downtown as a temporary employee. She was headed back to TSU for the fall semester. I would no longer be talking with her daily riding to and from work. I now feared losing her to some young college man with much more potential for financial success and far more worth to win her love. In my downward spiral, my emotions started to deceive me with the thought of me wanting her to have someone better than a loser like me. It would be back to being alone again. Again, raising its ugly head was that enemy of mine that visited to taunt my emotions.

> *Maybe she didn't really hear the Lord say that I was her husband and that is why she just left. No, that can't be it. Why can't I just beat down this feeling of rejection and abandonment? Am I PLAGUED??? No, I am strong and I can win this fight! I can't lose her! Here I go again, making stupid decisions costing me so much! Is there no end to this cycle? Agggghhh! I can win this fight. I can do this!*

Although I made several attempts that night to reach Denise by phone, she did not accept my call until the next day. I braced myself to hear the worst, but regardless of my fears, I was hoping there was a deposit of love in her heart and belief in our future together. In the tone of her voice I could tell there was hurt in her heart. It tore me in pieces knowing I had caused it. This was the first time we had ever been at odds with one another and it wasn't pretty. She spoke mildly, but in a very stern way, letting me know I was not getting away with what I had done. No sweet, smooth talking was going to ease this conversation over.

She asked me, "How could you do this? What else are you hiding? Do you not know how hard I have been striving to get my parents to accept you?" Then she asserted, "You have got to get your act together. I am not tolerating dishonesty in our relationship." And then the big one, "I need SPACE."

Have you ever been blasted in a nice kind of way? Though I was aware of her strength, she was much stronger than I anticipated. She had never spoken like this to me before, "Wow!" I felt awful. *I deserve every bit of this, but just give me a chance. Whatever you do please, don't walk away from me...it was a mistake! I didn't mean for this to happen! I'm being truthful about everything else, please don't hold this against me...I NEED you!!!* The entire conversation was intense, but there was hope.

Though there was an understandable degree of reluctance, she didn't distrust me altogether. At that moment, I desperately wanted something to help solidify our relationship and regain her trust. Within a month, I received an answer to my prayer, but it took faith to make it happen.

A Way Out of No Way

I received a call from a musician friend of mine who told me about a church that was looking to hire a piano player that would serve as the choir instructor and worship leader. This position required someone with the ability to "play by ear", which means to learn a song just by hearing it. He knew I was not a piano player, but I had told him once about the song that Denise had played for me. Of course, he had no idea that the song she played was the only Christian one she knew at the time. It would seem irrational to expect Denise to consider this opportunity.

So I told our musician friend something even more irrational. Denise and I together would audition for the worship leader position as a team. I had never taught or directed a choir, and becoming the worship leader for a church had never before come across my mind. *What a concept!* In retrospect, I have found that sometimes faith is fueled by need, whether the need is real or perceived. My motive was to place Denise with me in a situation of working closely together again and to impress her by providing an opportunity in which we both could make money. The audition was set. *Hmmmm. All there is now is to convince Denise.*

I would reason that since Denise had previously played for church youth in her early teenage years for a few months, and also had come from a musically inclined family. I was confident she would be successful in this position. Although she had only done this for a few months, teaching parts had always been a cinch for her due to the gift of harmony. Then of course, I as a saxophonist had played with bands led by excellent choir directors and worship leaders. I put the two ideas together and gathered that I would teach and direct the choir with her assistance as she focused on learning songs on the piano and supplying harmony parts for the choir.

Despite my brilliant plan, when I informed Denise of the position, she initially thought that I had lost my mind. We talked about it for about an hour as I challenged every excuse that she mentioned with a resolution. After much deliberation, my faith in what God could do through her on the piano must have gotten her attention. This intrigued her. After all it was what she witnessed her mother do her entire life and knew the family gift was within her. She suddenly stopped making excuses and began to see the possibilities of growing as an instrumentalist, and then agreed to do the audition.

The auditioning choir was highly motivated to hire someone. The congregation and pastor had grown weary of worship service without music. Choir members began smiling with excitement and whispering to one another as we entered the church. They had never seen a male and female serving as a worship leader team. We had prepared the only song Denise knew. Using a teaching technique I had learned from a former choir director in college and adding a bit of my own style, I taught the choir the song while Denise played. Whatever God had done with Denise's music the first time I heard it, He did it again with the choir.

They loved it! They believed like me, that she could replicate that sound on any song she learned. We were hired on the spot! Denise and I walked out of the church cool and calm. Once the door closed behind us, we quickly gave each other a big hug and rejoiced. The feel of her body embraced in my arms and mine in hers brought a sigh of relief to my heart. We had our work cut out for us, but working together side by side was all that mattered to me. This brought me such hope, as I knew God used this as a way of assuring her that we were meant to work together. We immensely enjoyed being together. I felt He had stamped what I perceived to be my plan with approval, but actually, I was unwittingly following His plan.

Just as I suspected it would, Denise's dexterity on the piano accelerated. She learned an art of reproducing almost any song she heard. If there was any part in a song that she didn't know well, I would cover it up by playing louder on my saxophone, because yes, I played and directed almost simultaneously. She would give me soprano, alto, and tenor parts for each song to teach the choir.

Through music we learned to work well with each other, though in reality I depended on her so much. I felt that this was true teamwork! A sense of unity began to take root in our hearts that was unbreakable. We didn't lead worship as two individuals. We led as one.

In a little over a year, our reputation extended to outside of our usual choir and we were widely received and requested by other churches. Sometimes other churches sent requests to hire us. On multiple occasions, we were asked to work with children and youth choirs, but fearing my past would be discovered and lack of desire to deal with the "horse playing" of children, adults were enough for me. Even Denise had her mind set on never working with children's choirs feeling as though it would be more work and take more patience. We made the decision not to ever work with children; even shook on it.

Please Let Her Be My Wife

I had fallen deeply in love with Denise. By the end of 1992, we began to discuss marriage. For me as a man, this was a frightening prospect financially. In my heart, I was torn between having the woman of my dreams and not being able to meet her expectations as a provider. Thoughts of being marked by a criminal record caused me to lose my temper and yell out to God in times of despair. I had finally started the church bulletin and typesetting business due in part to landing a $200 contract, and eventually made over $300 per week net. Still, our combined incomes with my temporary job and our worship leader check didn't amount to very much. Instead of depending on God for provision, I was trusting too much in my own abilities to earn money.

In spite of the circumstances, I decided it was time to propose to Denise. I couldn't afford a nice dinner with roses like I wanted. I purchased a very inexpensive engagement ring that nearly took a magnifying glass to see the diamond. There was nothing from romance books or movies requiring money that I could use to impress Denise. All I had was the truth of love in my heart for her. One quiet evening I got on one knee and asked Denise to marry me. As usual she gave me her humble smile and then responded, "Yes." Later, she found out that I had pawned the only thing that was of value to me, my saxophone, to purchase her ring. She told me that it made my proposal that much more of a treasure to her, because she knew by that gesture that I truly loved her with all of my heart.

We set our date to marry for July 1993 and began to plan the wedding. It was then that we encountered a major obstacle. Denise's parents knew that I had been incarcerated; yet they didn't on the other hand know that I had been in Brushy Mountain State Penitentiary. It wasn't something that I was hiding. It was just that it was never discussed. The detectives in them, however, led them to run a background check on me. They discovered my violent past and stint at Brushy Mountain. Her parents were so convinced in their suspicions about me having the potential to harm Denise, they refused to believe the reformation in my character. They didn't know that the final fight I had suffered against the tyrant was in self-defense and to protect myself and someone else.

With everything that Denise's family learned about me, they aggressively tried to stop our wedding, as they overwhelmingly feared for her safety. This was totally understandable for parents who loved their daughter. They wanted three assurances for their first born little girl as it pertained to marriage; they wanted her to have love, safety and provision. At the present time I was striking out at two of the three. Along with her parents finding out about my background, Denise was getting bombarded with complaints, speculations and reasons to retract her decision to marry me. She secretly asked God for a sign to marry me or not, hoping for the confirming voice she had heard before our relationship started. While all of this drama was still going strong, Denise invited me to dinner at a restaurant.

I was curious and afraid of this meeting. How could we stand against so much attack? I prayed for God to grant us grace to overcome this battle. After we finished our meals, Denise reached into her purse to get something for me. I thought, *Please don't let this be a "Dear John" letter.* It wasn't. She pulled out a small rectangular object with a cylindrical hole at the top. Inside the hole was a distinct line. The moment I saw the line, she said, "I'm pregnant." Her face was straight with no real expression, yet she looked nervous, as she waited for me to say something. Obviously, we had not been righteous in maintaining sexual purity. Yet, in our sin, God created a life full of His destiny. God would later use this as a lesson plan for us to learn unconditional love towards others.

The shock of the moment caused me to just look at her with my mouth slightly open. I gave my classic response when I don't know what to say, "Wow!" She began to apologize for all the obstacles that had recently waged against us. She explained that she never stopped believing what she wrote in the letter when we were just friends, that we would someday be happily married, but due to the latest events she began to waiver. She told me that she recently asked God for a sign of what He revealed over two years ago, that He would join us together in marriage. She realized that it was God undoubtedly answering this request. To her, there couldn't have been a more concrete way to seal His promise. You see, medically, neither Denise nor I should have been able to easily conceive a child without medical intervention of some kind. We both had physical issues that led us to doubt that children would be in our future. God hears and answers each request by each person in the way that is best in His eyes, not according to man's logic or precepts, so this is how he answered Denise. Despite all the obstacles and adversity, our priority became clear and we began to make arrangements to schedule the wedding sooner.

The Most Unlikely Job

We agreed that absolutely nothing was going to stop us from getting married. I decided to do the honorable thing and ask Denise's father for her hand in marriage. My only concern was that I needed more income, so before I approached her father, I searched the newspaper "Want Ads" and noticed a computer operator position at the corporate office of a large chain restaurant. I met the basic requirements of the position, but my criminal record was again the huge roadblock. Against all reason, I went to apply anyway.

My heart almost skipped a beat when the department head told me that the job required operating a mainframe computer that printed out all the checks for employees and the accounts payable department. I nearly laughed in the man's face when he explained the position. The shift was after business hours from 7:00 pm to 4:00 am with an unarmed guard on duty. It took award winning acting skills to keep my professional composure knowing the unlikelihood of getting this type of job with my criminal record. It was a definite conflict of interest, if you know what I mean!

The department head did not realize that a former computer hacking bank robber was applying for his job that required operating and trouble shooting a computer that printed out over ten million dollars of signed, cash-able checks each week. Sometimes life is full of irony, but God can also make life full of redemption. My resume' was twinkling with college training, computer programming tutorial jobs, and experience at Eastman Kodak.

Maybe my experience blinded the department head from reason, or maybe he just didn't do a background check that he said the job required. Whatever the case, he called me the next day and told me that I got the job! My voice began to slightly crack from heavy emotions of gratitude. As soon as he hung up the phone, I cried in appreciation to God, knowing only He could give me the gift of this job. Getting control of my emotions, I told Denise who was with me during the phone call. Her happiness for me, for us, caused me to tear up even more. To hide myself, I walked quickly to the bathroom and released a river of tears.

I went to Denise's dad a few months after getting the job to ask for her hand in marriage. It was then winter of 1992. He asked me every question in the "I- really-don't-want-you-as-my-son-in-law" book. Questions like: "Do you really think you can take care of my little girl." "When are you going to finish that college degree?" "Do you think you can make enough money to a raise a family?" I sweated and turned nervously in my seat at every question. Then he asked, "Do you love my daughter?" No degree of anxiousness, no fear of him, no doubt in the world stopped me from telling him boldly, "Absolutely YES." He did not show approval one way or the other. He just said, "You've done what you had to do." His response indicated that he knew, as well as I did that I was there as a demonstration of honor for him. He respected that. It had been my hope that upon meeting the woman I would marry, I would gain a father figure in my father in law. I walked away disappointed with his lack of joy, but not surprised by his reaction.

On July 31, 1993, Denise at three months pregnant and I were married in the flower garden of Centennial Park in Nashville, Tennessee. As an act of appreciation and love, the members of our first choir managed the reception after the wedding. As I reflect on that day I recall my pit of the stomach nervousness, but I was the happiest man on earth knowing that the woman designed specifically and perfectly for me was about to become my daily sunshine.

Can this be true? Am I dreaming? God, you have truly shined on me the love only You can give. I stand here at the alter, looking at the bridesmaids walking elegantly across the small garden bridge, one by one stepping down to join their escort. As each escort greeted a bridesmaid, he would hand her one single red rose and they would lock arms and walk together around the garden to their court place. Oh, I was so excited! Then the moment of my heart's desire arrived; I saw Denise strolling toward me from a different entrance of the garden. She had walked down the stairs to lock arms with her tall, stout escort; the one who would give her away to me, the one from whom I had longed to have approval...her father. This may now mean I will indeed have a real, tangible "Dad" in my life. The wind blew her long veil behind her in a mesmerizing flow as she passed each dazzling couple that pleasantly smiled when they gazed upon her. She was STUNNING! She was beautiful, as spectacular as the multicolored scenery of flowers that surrounded the garden. The fragrance of God's perfumed creation filled the air with every breath taken. All of my senses were heightened taking in every single detail of this moment. I wanted to remember it all for the rest of my life. As I glanced around, people from all over the park were rushing over to take pleasure in becoming spectators at our wedding. The music was remarkable as professional musicians and renowned singers of the city melodiously painted the atmosphere with the sound of love.

Yes, that sunny day was the day all my fears of losing her became naught. We were made one in the sight of God and ready to take on the world together, but we were going to need every ounce of unity in love that God would grant for the path He had set before us.

Chapter 8

IMPRISONED BY KIDNEY FAILURE

T he next year started out with a bang. Several days into January, we went to the hospital to give birth to our son. Denise had complications and could not give birth without surgery. I stood in the operating room and watched as Denise lie shaking from the epidural medication. This was one of the greatest feelings of helplessness in my life. As the doctor was lifting our baby boy through the incision, his head greeted the world with a loud cry even before the rest of his body was out. We named him Chazn, meaning leader of musicians and worship.

Kidding Around

Several months after the birth of our son, an amazing event took place as a newfound consideration for children touched our hearts. Our reputation as a musical duo had spread. In 1995, we got a request to help a children's choir at another church. This time I gave it some serious thought. The pastor and parents of the choir told me that no musicians wanted to work with the children. All the other musicians had the same type of excuses that Denise and I previously had: "The kids won't listen. I don't have time to babysit a bunch of kids. Kids don't sing as well as adults." The list went on and on.

Call it a crazy idea. Call it a burden from God. Call it a softening of my heart for the children. Whatever you call it, Denise and I had agreed a short time ago, that we would never get involved with children, yet here we were feeling compelled to take the position. We officially became the children's choir trainers and worship leaders on alternate weeks of the month for this second church, while continuing to work with the adults on our first church job.

The choir consisted of approximately thirty-five children mostly from ages six to twelve with a few teenagers. The location of the church was in a poor area of Nashville. We soon discovered that most of the kids did not have fathers in their homes. They would run up to me at every rehearsal and every other Sunday to give me a big hug as if they hadn't had one in weeks. Being in church every Sunday, Denise and I both learned more about God and became steadfast in the faith.

Working with the kids was never without a fun moment. As I directed and taught the choir, some kids would sing as loud as their little lungs would let them. Others would just stand there and stare at me. We learned some important factors that apply only to children, such as, it didn't matter whether they made a mistake or not! When adults made mistakes, the congregation would frown in disapproval, but when the kids made mistakes the congregation would think, "That's so cute." I believe the kids knew we cared for them. We treated them as if they were our own children. They would sing like they never had before. The children's choir gained such recognition that the pastor stopped taking his adult choir on speaking invitations and took the children's choir instead. They were amazing.

In the spring of 1996, Denise and I were learning to be parents. Life was going fairly well financially with our small family and we had moved into a larger apartment. I had tried to develop various small businesses only to lose money each time. My job was eliminated due to corporate restructuring. I had gotten a job with the Tennessee State Department of Finance and Administration. We still had revenue coming in from my church bulletin business and receiving money from both churches. We were still not quite in middle class status, but we were growing.

While reading the Bible one morning in early summer of 1996, I got the urge deep in my heart to stop allowing money to be my primary motive. I felt that my goal was to surrender to God and trust Him for financial provision in whatever ministry He chose for us. I guess that would be called "full-time" ministry. There's an old song that says, "You can't beat God giving...the more you give the more He gives to you" and this is exactly how we wanted to live life. I was excited about the prospect of giving our all to the work of the Lord. It felt so purposeful and brought immeasurable peace. My physical health seemed to be great. I was full of energy jumping up and down with the kids in the choir and playing with our two-year-old son. Then Denise brought the rectangular device with the cylindrical hole to me again. Yes, we were pregnant with our second child. Life was getting better and better.

Big Legs - Big Problem

When mid-August rolled around, I awoke one morning and noticed my legs larger than usual. Unsure of how long they had been larger, I didn't think much about it. I always wanted larger legs. My upper body had been proportionately in shape, but my legs needed a little help in size. Larger legs made me feel that I was more attractive to my wife. For the first few days of my new legs, I purposely wore shorts to show my physique. My trivial desire to show off my new impressive legs was blinding me from seeing a warning sign of a potentially dangerous problem.

For over a week, my legs and my feet had gradually

swollen larger and larger until I could no longer fit in my shoes and could barely walk. The swelling was definitely fluid retention, a symptom that warranted immediate medical attention. On August 22, 1996, on my 35th birthday I checked into General Hospital, without any medical insurance. For days, the doctors prescribed medication to reduce the fluid in my body without the ability to properly diagnose the source of the swelling.

My cholesterol level went astronomically high revealing itself as another threatening warning sign. Nurses would come to see me wondering how I was fairing being so close to congestive heart failure from the high cholesterol. My blood pressure also was abnormally high. At that point, I became very worried not knowing the mysterious cause of my symptoms. With the exception of the poisonous snakebite as a boy, I had never stayed overnight as a hospital patient. As much as I hated having to be away from my family, I was admitted for two weeks. At the point of spending two straight weeks in the hospital, I ended up missing a couple of choir rehearsals with the children's choir. Several of the kids had their parents bring them to visit me at the hospital praying that I would get better.

I was released two weeks later without a proper diagnosis of the problem. General Hospital was the medical facility that cared for patients without insurance, yet the bill for my medical stay was enormous. Fluid retention pills were the only medication prescribed on my release. As the days progressed, my physical strength went into a gradual decline. Within a couple of weeks of my hospital release, I returned to the General Hospital clinic. This time I was referred to a Nephrologist, a doctor who specializes in treating disorders and diseases of the kidney.

For Real?

The Nephrologist scheduled a renal biopsy for the

following week. She told me that a renal biopsy was the removal of a small piece of kidney tissue for examination. I said, "Remove what?!" Remove meant that she was going to cut out a little piece of my kidney to test for disease. This was getting much too serious.

What on earth had I done to cause this? Have I done something wrong, God? Surely someone as healthy as I was couldn't have a disease.

Anxiously, I recited my normal diet to convince the Nephrologist that there must be some type of mistake. I assured her that everything was going to turn out okay. I regularly drank plenty of water and few sodas. There was no history of kidney disease with my parents. Though my blood pressure was high when I was admitted to the hospital, I had no personal history of high blood pressure or diabetes, the two most common causes of kidney disorders.

This all had to be a terrible mistake. I love God, and I work for Him. They are mistaking me for someone else...must have been a mix up with the records.

In the week prior to the renal biopsy, Denise and I went to practice with the children's choir. Regardless of my extremely weak state, I forced myself to go. The kids would unknowingly hurt my fragile body as they hugged me tight as usual. My heart was encouraged as the kids greeted me with words of support, "Are you going to be all right Mr. Joe? If you go back to the hospital I want to spend the night with you. Did you like the food in there? What was that tube sticking out of your arm?" Oh, the innocence of the children made me long for more faith. They didn't know how afraid

I was, but they reassured me. They didn't know how alone I felt inside, but they comforted me. They weren't aware of my guilty conscious, yet their affection assured me I was in the will of God. I felt so much genuine love and concern flowing from their little hearts, and it strengthened me every time I was with them. The days leading up to the biopsy seemed more like weeks.

The day for the renal biopsy finally arrived. Denise, about four months pregnant, and our little son waited for me, while the doctor did the biopsy. At the end of the procedure the doctor asked that I return in a few days for the results. During that waiting period, Denise kept praying and remaining faithful. Her faith in the Lord had tremendously grown in the time that we had been married. We didn't know how or why we were facing such a dire situation, but she would not be shaken. I, in contrast, started confessing and repenting from everything in my memory that I had done wrong and felt.

The day came and our small family went with a degree of hope to get the renal biopsy results. As we sat in the doctor's office waiting, Chazn sat quietly in my lap as Denise prayed again. The doctor sighed as she sat down as if she had something important to say. She looked me in the eye and said, "Mr. Bradford we have the results back from your biopsy. The tests did not come back as I had hoped, but I will explain the conditions and treatment of the test results. You have been diagnosed with a kidney disease called Focal Segmental Glomerulosclerosis. It's called FSGS in the short form. This is..." I stopped the doctor in mid-sentence and asked her, "Now what did you just say?" She repeated the name of the kidney disease.

The name of the disease alone was longer than any sickness I had ever heard. Denise and I calmly braced ourselves to hear the rest of the diagnosis. The doctor then said, "FSGS is a rare kidney disease that destroys the function of the kidneys. The cause is still unknown to modern medicine. I'm sorry to inform you, but more than half of those with this disease will develop chronic kidney failure within ten years."

Am I Going To Die?

Maybe I would be in the fraction of patients that don't get kidney failure. This statistic gave me a little hope. Then the doctor said, "I'm very sorry Mr. Bradford. The disease is for some unknown reason very aggressive in your body's system. At its rate of progression your kidneys will fail in less than three years." Denise and I were stunned. All we could do was gasp. I didn't know what to say, but I had many questions running through my mind.

> *Did this mean that I would die and leave my family alone? Could Denise raise our little ones? Would they remember me as their father?*

This fear was stimulated as I thought of leaving them without support; a condition I know all too well. I can't leave them. They need me! From my inward cry of mercy and fighting back tears, I eagerly asked the doctor, "What does this all mean?" The doctor assured us that there was hope. With proper treatment my kidneys would possibly last a little longer. When and if my kidneys did fail, it would be absolutely necessary to get a kidney transplant or be placed on a dialysis machine to avoid death. The doctor prescribed blood pressure and fluid retention medications along with steroids and other drugs. I was placed on a special diet that included low fluid intake, low salt, low cholesterol, and low fat. We left the doctor's office in a daze, unable to totally comprehend what just took place. I can't begin to fully express the feeling I had inside. I had thought I'd been through every emotion there was. I was terribly wrong. It was one of those moments where I had no answers, no comprehension, and very little hope. As I walked out, I could feel the squeeze of Denise's hand getting tighter and tighter. Sometimes a touch is more than any word spoken. From that time forward, reliance on my own power ended, and training in trusting only in God for *everything* had to begin.

Disease immediately took a heavy toll on our financial status. Our only income came from my bulletin business and positions as worship leaders. I remember our electricity bill being at the point of being suspended from an inability to pay the bill. Defeat overcame me, as time after time I would think:

> *This one I can't control. This one I can't fix. I am completely helpless and can't even protect my own family. This can't be me? Am I in my own body? I had never been sick before and now boom out of nowhere...WHY? WHYYYY God???? If it weren't for this Samurai fighter within, I would certainly give up.*

The fate of my family seared every thought of my mind. I had little choice. To support my family, I was forced to apply for every type of financial assistance available for the very poor. Though physically weak I drove to a State agency to apply for emergency assistance and waited there nearly two hours with barely enough strength to sit up. It was a great humbling experience waiting in a room filled with other impoverished people seeking assistance. Great gloom and despair filled the entire room, as worn sad faces stared into nothing. Children needing baths ran around seeking attention from anyone who would give it. I did not feel encouraged at all there. In fact I continually wondered WHY I was there in the first place. NEVER in my living days would I have *ever* thought I would be there. Yet, something inside told me that I must trust God. There must be a strategic plan of His in the works.

Chemical reactions in my body were out of control. The medications didn't seem to be helping. At one moment I would be standing cooking scrambled eggs, the next moment I was yelling for Denise to take the eggs off the stove while I crawled over to the chair. Sometimes lying on the hard floor was the solution to resist panic mode in my mind. The steroids were causing me to overeat resulting in acid reflux keeping me awake at night. In spite of overeating, I was still quickly losing weight, because the disease was causing a heavy loss of protein in my blood. I was trapped in a body of chaos. Many times I looked down at my son and wondered what it would be like to not see him grow up.

It was January 1997. The Nephrologist had predicted three years, but in three months I was at the point of kidney failure. No degree of martial arts could defeat this foe. No defensive maneuver I had used to protect others and myself in prison could have any effect against this enemy. Night after night I read books and articles to find something that would work against this disease, but nothing existed in the natural world. I felt my life helplessly being drained from me. *Am I really going to die?* Denise would always assure me that God would not call me to do His work and then take me on to glory before I could get started. This was my ray of hope. I believed my purpose had not yet been fulfilled. *But how?* I had nothing, except a tiny spec of faith. My faith was in her faith. Simply put, I believed in her faith that I would be okay and that I would NOT die.

I had applied for federal disability in the fall of 1996, to get money to support my family and more importantly to get Medicare for dialysis surgery. I was initially rejected. We couldn't believe it, so we appealed because it was clear to me that my near future was either dialysis or death.

Nevertheless, as we went through the appeal process, which took months, God provided for us in miraculous ways as our church family and unexpected people would give money and/or food without knowing of our dire situation. Our hearts were moved and given new perspective on others who didn't have resources for necessities.

Delivery Room Drama

On February 14, 1997, we rushed Denise to the hospital to give birth to our second child. We prayed and believed for a normal delivery. Another surgical delivery would cause Denise to be temporarily helpless. This would be a problem, as I needed her strength to be able to help me at home. As Denise sat in the delivery room, she success-fully dilated more and more. I sat in a chair beside her bed. My weight had gone from 152 pounds to 119 pounds since September of the previous year. Regardless of my near death frail state, I was eager to meet my new baby girl.

As Denise was at the point of being fully dilated to have the baby, the nurses and doctor came running in. Suddenly, a jolt of pain hit my chest unlike any I had ever experienced. It felt like someone took a double hammer and whacked me on both sides of my chest at the same time. I fell back in my chair in total shock. Not wanting to draw attention I whispered, "What was that?" The nurses were quickly pre-paring the bed covering and getting Denise in position to give birth. The lead nurse said, "She's fully dilated!"

I moved to stand up and again a powerful jolt of pain hit my chest harder than the first, this time knocking me to my knees. Five seconds later, another jolt hit knocking me flat on the floor. Then the jolts started gyrating my body every second. Each time this jolt hit I felt like my heart would stop. Not wanting to stress Denise in the midst of childbirth, I fought to crawl to the door. A nurse noticed me and called for a man to help me out of the door. As

I was dragged out of the room, I noticed Denise's doctor checking for the baby's head.

An emergency medical team came rushing to me with a stretcher. Still gyrating from the spasms, I was placed on a stretcher. OHHHH, the pain! I didn't know what hurt more, this excruciating pain or the pain of missing my daughter's birth. As I was taken to the emergency room, I prayed, "Lord, please don't take me now. Please let me see my little girl. Please let me be a daddy to the kids you blessed me with. Please Lord, let me stay and be a husband to Denise." Five minutes after I arrived at the emergency room, the powerful jolts stopped. The diagnosis was not a heart attack. I had experienced massive muscle spasms due to a loss of protein in my blood. After observation in the emergency room I went back to the delivery room and met our new baby girl. We named her Caylin, which means a girl that is pure.

After a few weeks I was blessed with medical insurance. This was major to me, because the specialist and surgery that I needed would have been nearly impossible for us to afford. Now that it was in place it allowed the Vanderbilt doctors to give me surgery for peritoneal dialysis.

I was now imprisoned to a kidney machine for nine of the 24 hours in a day. I was distraught, but I was alive. . . .

Chapter 9

MINISTRY ON A MACHINE

꽃

A major new factor of life on the dialysis machine at home was dealing with daily pain. The dialysis process itself would give me light stomach cramps each day at a particular point in the procedure. Various agonizing symptoms were associated with FSGS. The aches and pains were relentless throughout each day. It was only a matter of where they would hit next. To get my mind off my daily plight of pain I searched for a new hobby. I decided to try reading the Bible again. It was slow at first. Television would normally win out. I often thought about Solomon who wrote the Book of Proverbs. I found a verse that would stick with me through any sickness:

> *"The spirit of a man will sustain him in sickness, but who can bear a broken spirit?"*
> *(Prov. 18:14)*

The Right Attitude

This unyielding sickness that placed me on the dialysis machine nearly broke my spirit causing me to want to give up. In this verse, I saw that God could give me an attitude of victory in any situation of sickness. I really needed that truth. The warrior within my heart had fought with physical strength all my life. Now through the power of the Holy

Spirit I had to fight from within. From the onset of the disease, I would periodically tell Denise that God was not going to take me home with Him yet, and that He had some purpose for me here joined with her, to bring up our children and for something more not yet known.

Before reaching the goal of our purpose together, this disease was going to try our character. It was going to try our faith and trust in God. The bridges were burned behind us. We could not go back to "normal" life, as we knew it. We were forced to allow God to grow a strong spirit within us to be useful to Him regardless of what seemed to be improbable or impossible in this physical natural earth. We did not know what attacks this destructive disease would try next, but "dog gone it" with Christ in the center of our union, victory would be the outcome.

Adjustment To Life on a Machine

Life on a dialysis machine took an incredible adjustment. I always wanted to be the Bionic Man, but this was ridiculous. The surgeons had placed a permanent flexible hollow foot long tube in my abdomen for peritoneal dialysis. About 5 inches of the tube extended out from my body. I was required to use this tube to hook up to the machine everyday around 5:30 p.m. for an hour. Then at night between 10:00 - 11:00 pm, I had to hook up to the machine nonstop for 8 hours. Imagine that! God forbid that our apartment would catch on fire!

Nevertheless, we still had an active lifestyle. We were caring for our newborn daughter and our three year old son. We kept our church bulletin business going, and continued as worship leaders of the adult choir as well as the children. The unfortunate part about all of this was, we couldn't travel freely with the machine. Wherever we went "it" went. I recall a time we flew to Cleveland, Ohio. I treated that machine like it was my youngest baby! "Be careful", "Don't hurt it", "Watch out don't hit the wall!" I couldn't imagine what would happen if something happened to it. Upon arriving at the airport we couldn't find it. Talk about panic! I thought, *Well, this is it...the end of our trip and we just got here.* Eventually we got word that it had been put on "delay" and it was coming but on a different plane. That mistake caused enormous concern for us! I had missed my evening treatment, which resulted in contaminated fluid filling up my whole peritoneal cavity. I felt so uncomfortable I thought I would explode from suffocation. We were put at ease when we later picked it up that night. What a trip!

From the start of dialysis, Denise had the task of aiding, comforting, and encouraging me while nurturing a new baby girl and our son. There was an intricate sterile procedure for preparing and connecting the tube in my abdomen to the dialysis machine. With one simple mistake, a single germ could get inside the dialysis tube connected to my body. If that happened, an infection called "peritonitis" could develop and spread like wildfire inside of me within minutes requiring immediate medical attention. Knowing the danger of this infection, Denise's concern as a loving wife would often cause her to ask if I needed assistance, but the procedure was designed primarily for me to do alone. I could so deeply feel her compassion for me in such a challenging situation.

Ministry At Home

Ministry, for Denise and I, had always started first at home. We had to learn how to cope with the invasion of a daily dialysis machine. Managing common household chores and little children while on a machine took much "patience" training.

The machine and all its tubes were captivating to our three-year-old son, which was not a good thing for me. A tube coming out of daddy's stomach tied to a machine just didn't seem natural to him. So, he tried to help me by pulling the tube out of my stomach. I learned to hold him warmly in my arms and explain the rules of not hurting daddy. As time went on, hooking up to the machine meant that daddy was going to give him a big hug.

As much as I was beginning to cherish children, one of my greatest nightmares was a house full of kids while I was on the machine. One of our closest family friends had several small children. Each time they would visit, I tried hard to convince the kids that Mr. Joe did not have the machine out for "show and tell." The kids always had the urge to analyze the workings of the machine while I was connected to it, but when their hands began grabbing tubes they seemed like miniature mad scientists to me. My best defensive strategy to save myself from the kids that loved me so much was to have them visit when I was off the machine.

God gave us much grace with our baby girl. She was abnormal in a wonderful kind of way. She rarely would cry out loud when I was in bed on the machine. To avoid feeling stomach cramps, it was necessary for me to be in a deep sleep at certain times in the dialysis process. Hours of deep sleep for a parent in a bedroom with a hungry baby are normally a paradox, but whenever baby Caylin wanted her mother, she would only give a little pant, alerting Denise's quick response. Denise and I both had to be blind to not see what was happening. The quietness of a newborn baby at night, which seemed unimportant on the list of concerns for the average parent, was such an enormous gift of love from God to me.

Learning Mercy From A Child

Serving as worship leaders for the children's choir took on a whole new look. The children heard that I had been placed on a dialysis machine, and could not wait to ask me about it. It was fun seeing the many ways that the word "dialysis" could be pronounced from the mouth of a child: "Mr. Joe, are you really on a 'ditilis' machine." "What's that 'ditatalis' machine look like?" "Did the doctor give you that 'dialactic' machine free, or did you have to pay for it?" The innocence of the children was actually feeding my spirit to fight on. I found it so humorous. I couldn't help but laugh regardless of how much I did not want to be on that machine. To be in the midst of pureness and joy was like heaven to me. "Let the little children come to Me...for of such is the kingdom of heaven." (Matt. 19:14) I was gaining new perspective that somehow outweighed the pressures coming against me.

Children are sometimes more observant than many adults give them credit. Denise and I transported musical equipment whenever we did rehearsal or worship with the kids. We had to load and unload a 72 key semi-heavy electronic piano, a portable piano stand, a large amplifier, a saxophone, and a bag of electric and music cords. Unfortunately, grown-ups who knew of my weak predicament would often not notice that the equipment was loading me down. On the other hand, kids would run up to me regularly offering to carry the equipment. The children's intuition was greatly appreciated.

It was not apparent to me at first, but while I was weak from the dialysis machine at rehearsals and worship services, all along the children were being used as instruments in lessons of mercy. I learned so much by watching them. Little kids would hold my hand and pull me up the stairs of the church entrance. They would run downstairs and get me a cup of water when thirsty. At times they would even debate over whose turn it was to help me. They were my little helpers simply because they loved me and knew I needed them. This was so refreshing each time we were together. What a parabolic lesson it was to learn through children.

Peritonitis

For a year the transitions on a dialysis machine were challenging, but manageable. Then the thing that I had hoped to avoid finally happened. Germs got into the peritoneal tube and migrated inside my body. The dialysis fluid that was recycled out of my body was normally a clear to pale yellow color. On this occasion, the fluid had a sort of cloudy color. Fluid is always replaced back into the peritoneal cavity covering the stomach area. I was eager to see the color of the fluid every single time it was recycled out of my body in hopes it would be clear. In a matter of minutes, I began to feel sharp needle like pains in my stomach area accompanied by nausea.

As the pain increased it was obvious that an intense peritonitis infection was imminent. Unable to move or stand on my feet, I called out for Denise. To see a sign of how far the infection had advanced, I recycled the fluid out of my body before the required amount of treatment time. The color of the fluid had reached a frightening thick cloudy consistency suggesting a fast growing infection. Immediately, she called for the ambulance. Our little son stood in the hallway in disarray unable to understand why daddy was moaning and unable to walk without falling.

As we heard the ambulance coming, Denise amazingly kept calm. She placed the baby on the bed and came to assist me, knowing I had to disconnect from the machine before I could be taken in the ambulance. Weighing much more than me due to my illness, she used her body weight to support me as she leaned me on her shoulder. She pulled the machine as she walked me into the master bedroom bathroom. Chills from the infection had set in. She quickly grabbed a blanket to cover me as she disconnected the tube from the machine.

We heard the knocks of the paramedics. She ran to let them in leading them to me in the master bedroom. I had managed to crawl out of the bathroom and lay in agony on the bed. Together two paramedics got on each side of me and practically carried me to the stretcher. Any movement would incite sharp pains around my stomach area. This was much to my displeasure, because the ambulance was one of the roughest riding vehicles imaginable for my condition.

Once in the hospital, heavy doses of the most common pain medications were immediately administered, however, they only eased the stinging that covered the expanse of my stomach. They did not stop it. Quickly the doctor had nurses start antibiotics. A dialysis machine was brought in the emergency room. I was hoping the pain would reduce when the machine recycled the fluid from my body. The withdrawal of the fluid in my body caused a degree of throbbing that caused me to verbally cry out to God. I kept repeating, *"This will pass. This will pass. This will pass…"* I fell asleep from sheer exhaustion. They admitted me to the hospital to fight the infection.

That experience tested my faith. Anger overwhelmed me. Questions that could not change my situation were flooding my mind.

> *Why God? Why? I don't understand your ways? I didn't want this awful disease. I didn't want this relentless infection. What had I done to deserve it? Okay, hold on and keep a good attitude. Believe for the best. I've got a family to love and support. There are children in the choir expecting me to return for hugs and quality time with music. God hasn't left you. Get yourself together!*

When Denise picked me up from the hospital, the joy of seeing her face caused me to sigh with relief. She never said a word that caused me to doubt that God would help me overcome any situation. When I say that my faith thrived off of hers, this is an understatement! I could tell she wanted me to release the emotional and mental stress and pain within me, but I just couldn't. She believed that God could heal me, but there were too many pinned up emotions to verbalize. All I could say was spoken through tears. For a man who had so much self-righteous pride before, trusting in my own power for survival, I struggled daily to not feel wimpy or weak. This was the last thing I wanted Denise to think of me. Yet, God humbled me to allow my genuine emotions to show, for I could no longer hide them.

Three months had gone by since being infected. Everyday, I took every precaution fearing the worst would happen again; I had to ensure a sterile connection to the dialysis machine to avoid peritonitis. However, there was another ailment that took me by surprise. I was accustomed to light pains throughout my body, but on this particular day, a jolt of pain struck me on a side where one of my kidneys was located. Minutes later a dull continuous pain started just above my groin. It was substantial and wouldn't stop. Denise got the kids together and took me to the hospital. The doctors diagnosed me with kidney stones, which are one of the most painful afflictions known to humans.

There are times in life when a person wonders if they can bear anything more, yet God knows exactly how much we can. Often, Denise and I were close to being evicted from our apartment home, while ailments from the disease kept us on our knees praying. Without kidney function, I rarely urinated. Without urine, calcium deposits began to regularly build up in my urinary tract causing kidney stones and regular visits to the emergency room.

As we worked with the children in choir, I felt purpose in the midst of so much despair. It was energizing to see little ones without a care in the world. One day as Denise and I were teaching the kids a new song, I took a deep breath to sing a part that took a lot of air. It felt like a knife cut me just above my navel. The pain hit each time I would breathe in. The kids saw me bend over holding my belly. To not alarm them, I pretended like nothing was wrong and withstood the pain to complete the rehearsal.

The pain above my navel would not go away for days. Then peritonitis struck me again. I had tried hard to avoid it. In the midst of preparing to rush to the hospital, the dull pain of a kidney stone also hit me. I thought, *No way! This could not be happening: peritonitis and kidney stones at the same time!* When I got to the emergency room, my strength was totally depleted. I was diagnosed not only with kidney stones and peritonitis. The doctors also discovered an umbilical hernia. The pressure of the fluid in my peritoneal cavity had caused my muscle to split open under my belly button. The infection and pain from all three ailments were nearly unbelievable. I was forced to be in a state of complete dependence on God for strength, hope, and dear life!

Admitted into the hospital overnight, my blood pressure went dangerously low. In and out of consciousness, I petitioned God for more of His mercy. He allowed me to make it through the traumatic night. The doctors had me go to the surgery room for a urinary tract probe for viewing and to clear any kidney stones. I was taken to the surgery room on another day to repair the hernia. The ride home with Denise after the complete hospital stay caused me to break down in tears. It was so tiring to be continually battling against sickness and disease.

When I held my kids, I thought, *No! I will not give up! If I can't do this for myself, God help me, I will do it for my kids!* Refusing to have a broken spirit, I was not yet out of danger from the terrible experience. The antibiotics were unable to completely destroy the infection. I was rushed back to the hospital within a few days. The doctors diagnosed aggressive bacteria that had connected itself to the tube inside my body. The only course of action was to remove the tube surgically.

Hemo!

There was a high degree of concern in cutting the tube out. I could no longer take peritoneal dialysis. The only way to keep me alive now would be hemodialysis, which filters the blood through an artificial kidney. Denise and I braced ourselves for another change in life. Hemodialysis could not be done at home. A common challenge with hemodialysis is having a working shunt (an access in the body to perform dialysis) in which to stick two large needles to recycle the blood.

After removing the peritoneal tube from my abdomen, the doctors had to perform hemodialysis in my groin. Words cannot express the anguish that came with having large needles stuck in my groin while I watched all my blood circulate from my body through a little artificial kidney. I felt, *"Now, they've done it all to me. Is there an end to this madness?!*

The next day the surgeons placed a temporary shunt just below my neck. A shunt located in this area of a patient was commonly known to get dangerous and sometimes deadly infections. After a few weeks the doctors performed surgery for a permanent shunt. After the procedure, I was told that there was a 50/50 chance it would work. The first one did not work. This was so freaky to be in such a terrible position and be told that the very thing that is to save my life...didn't work. We had to reschedule for another procedure. The second procedure was a success. I went home with a tube inside my arm that would forever remind me of one of the most dramatic life threatening fights in which I had ever been.

Hemodialysis required me to travel Monday, Wednesday, and Friday to a Vanderbilt dialysis clinic to sit on a machine for four hours each visit. I no longer required the use of the peritoneal dialysis machine, which I had been using for 15 months. So my son and daughter had to say goodbye to the machine for good and now goodbye to daddy several times a week. The frequent travel provided its own challenges as at times our vehicle would not work. When this happened, I had to take a long ride on a city bus to the dialysis clinic.

During each medical challenge, Denise would continue to serve as a worship leader without me. In 1998, we were offered a position to become children's choir worship leaders with one of Nashville's fastest growing African American churches. Around the same time, the church of our first group of kids got a new worship leader that agreed to work with their adults and children choir programs. This gave us peace, and we felt led by God to take the new position, since we had been seeking wisdom to become active members of that particular church for several weeks.

Our life then included hemodialysis and a worship leader position that required ministering weekly with over 80 kids under the age of 13 years. We soon found that the combination of hemodialysis and the new church was a divine plan to bridge us into an additional form of ministry.

Chapter 10

FROM TRANSPLANT TO
A. C. T. I. O. N.

A t the end of 1998, my weekly life had become defined
as life on a machine and life in ministry. I longed to
see a day when life on a machine was over. My doctors suggested that I consider being placed on a kidney transplant
list. A kidney transplant would get me off the machine, but
carried its own set of precautions and dangers, nevertheless,
anything would be better to me than living on a machine.
A kidney transplant would allow Denise and I to focus and
grow in whatever the Lord had planned for us in ministry. I
was unaware that life was about to take a twist while on a
hemodialysis machine to bridge us into a new ministry.

Dialysis Education 101
The hemodialysis machine differed from peritoneal
dialysis, which affected our weekly lifestyle. Hemodialysis
was a four-hour procedure done three times a week versus
the daily and nightly routine of the peritoneal dialysis.
Hemodialysis was performed at Vanderbilt while peritoneal dialysis was a home-based procedure. Hemodialysis
required being pierced by two of the largest needles used
in modern medicine to circulate the blood through an artificial kidney, while peritoneal dialysis involved connecting

to the machine with an implanted tube.

If there was any good that came out of the hemodialysis treatments, it was the relationships I enjoyed with other dialysis patients. No longer was I doing dialysis alone. The Vanderbilt dialysis clinic was a room full of dialysis machines, each with its own personal little adjustable television and earphones. The machines were connected side-by-side throughout the room with some machines in the middle of the room. One could watch television for the time they were there or talk with other patients seated beside and in front of him.

One good thing about the dialysis center was the moral support and information shared between patients. In my first visits, I learned that there were multiple causes of kidney failure and most of the patients were African American. I was told that the two most common causes of kidney failure, high blood pressure and diabetes, were more typical in African Americans than any other race. These statistics were repeated to me many times by the patients themselves. I guess they wanted to educate me, since I was the new kid on the block. Most of them were middle-aged to 70 years old, with the exception of a very few who were younger than I.

Unforgettable Faces

Seeing the damaging affects of diabetes in a dialysis clinic was also unavoidable. The whole room got a big laugh at my expense one day when I was seated directly facing one of the most notable characters in the clinic.

This guy was approximately forty years old, came in for treatment one hour after me, and sat in the empty chair facing me. He seemed to be a nice guy and appeared physically as normal as anyone else in the clinic. He began a conversation with me as he sat down. The nurse came and placed two large needles in a shunt in his arm and hooked him up to the hemodialysis machine.

The nice guy talked about sports and his kids. One of his favorite memories was athletics. Apparently, he had been involved in basketball and other sports as a teenager. He searched for sports on his television as we spoke. I made a suggestion that one day maybe we could meet at the basketball court and shoot a few hoops. After saying that, I heard a few little laughs coming from neighboring patients that were eaves dropping on our conversation. The nice guy just looked at me and smiled.

A few minutes later, he reached down, rolled up his pants and pulled off his left leg from the knee down. I was shocked! It was an artificial leg. I took in a deep breath and held it for a moment to help me keep my composure. I needed something to say quickly to redeem myself from my suggestion. He gracefully came to the rescue of my honor by mentioning the Special Olympics, though he had never competed himself. He said that dialysis patients qualified to compete in various athletic categories including wheelchair basketball. He informed me that many of the wheelchair basketball players had lost both of their legs. Then in awe, I watched him reach down, roll up his pants, and pull off his right leg from the knee down. I again was in shock! His right leg was also artificial.

It never dawned on me that I would be meeting other patients with medical challenges worse than mine. From that point on, I attentively listened to the many testimonies of victory that God had done to save the lives and encourage the people in that room. The nice guy in front of me told me that he formerly led a wild life of drinking, drugs, and sex with multiple women. He ignored the doctor's warnings of diabetes. After diabetes progressed in his body, he lost his legs and kidney function and could no longer follow his old lifestyle. Then confined to a dialysis machine he was humbled to repent from years of reaping destruction on his life and others'.

Another patient receiving dialysis was a beautiful, kind lady in her late sixties who looked as if she had been a pageant contestant in her younger years. After each of my treatment visits, I stopped by her chair to talk with her. She would share stories of her wonderful life, and she was prayerful that God would do the same for others. Not wishing to go into a nursing home as her family wished, she was adamant that she would live at home and teach her grandchildren to follow the ways of the Lord. Her encouraging attitude was pleasantly addictive. She called me son as if she had known me for years. I welcomed it, especially with my grandmother being gone.

Since patients were required to sit in the same seat each visit, it offered an added sense of security and normalcy that we all needed. There was a gentleman who was extremely loud, sitting just to my left. He said he was a Christian, but he criticized *everything*. When a doctor would come into the dialysis clinic telling the patients of new kidney transplant technology, he would contend against everything the doctor said. He suggested the surgeons might slip while doing the transplant surgery and kill him. He didn't want to take the many medications of a transplant patient. There was something negative to be gleaned from everything relating to his condition or treatment, yet his disposition changed when we talked about his church. He was head deacon, and said he loved the Lord and never missed a Sunday service, yet he did not allow that love to bring hope to himself or others. If the other patients had not discerned his critical attitude, then no one would have signed the list to get a kidney transplant.

Another interesting character in the clinic was an AIDS patient. He truly wanted to know God in a deeper way. He was one of the few patients in the self-help area of the clinic. He would stick himself with the two large needles and get his dialysis machine started without the help of a nurse. He was comfortable using needles, because he had been a drug addict. He had told us that the biggest regret in his life that caused him to contract AIDS was with an infected needle used by another drug addict. One day I introduced him to Denise. After that day she would sit with him at times and he would preach a 1970's small country town black Baptist preacher's sermon to her and others in the room, in conversation form of course.

It was eye opening to see how Jesus would reside in what could have been a place of great despair. Each dialysis session would bring more testimonies as I met various patients in the clinic. Many family members of the patients could not bare coming into the clinic. Apparently, the machines that purified people's blood overtly by withdrawing it and returning it again turned them off. So, as a result of this, patients consoled one another in a way that family and friends could not.

Characters In A Play

It was always a mission to find something to occupy the time when on the dialysis machine. Just as a thought, I began placing the various patients around me as characters in a play. I would then add fictional characters to complete a scene. I first looked at the loud Christian man to my left since he talked more than anyone else and realized how much his mind was in a box of misunderstanding concerning the role of a Christian. He thought that being a Christian meant coming to Sunday morning service and acting as good as possible, and then returning to a world of selfishness and criticism the rest of the week.

Using the loud man's attitude as inspiration, I thought of a short 20-minute play called "Get Out of the Box" and named his character, "The Sunday Morning Christian." Then I thought of other false mindsets that people believe about Christianity and I made characters based on their mindsets. Once staged, I wrote each character acting in their own personal cardboard box representing their mindset and wrote a dialogue between them and a monologue in which each one states his off track belief.

During my dialysis treatment, I completed the whole script for the short play, "Get Out of the Box" within a few short weeks. Writing the script was only the first part. As I wrote the play God was placing music in my head to go with it. How exhilarating this was for me. It was as though God had allotted this special time for me to explore the world of creativity in ways I never thought possible. He can use anything He chooses for His good. I thought back on when I was in solitary confinement, "the hole" for forty days begging God to give me an imagination to help me escape reality. That was to no avail. Now I wasn't doing anything at all to escape this "hole" of horrible physical ailment. However, I could vividly see how I was exactly where I was supposed to be and this brought such peace to my soul.

I told Denise that I had been writing plays while on the dialysis machine, and wanted her help with the music. She gave me one of those, "what-in-the-world-are-you-talking-about-*now*" looks. She saw the eagerness in my eyes to transform the plays into musical theater. It wasn't everyday that a husband would come presenting to his wife a play he wrote while on a dialysis machine. I thought back to the very beginning of our marriage. We were ready to conquer the whole world with God on our side, no matter what it looked or seemed like. I just knew anything was possible with God! All along I had thought it was her love carrying me, but in actuality it was His love for me through her supporting me. Being reminded of this gave me encouragement to pursue this endeavor with God.

I began to study all types of books on musical theater. I learned that writing scripts was only a part of a musical theater production. My goal was to learn everything I could about this field of creative arts. I studied lighting, sound, wardrobe, scenery, props, stage management, and all the components of musical theater. Administrating the whole production would mean to study other producers who were successful. I found several library books by play producers, which I consumed with great excitement.

With all the positive emotional energy that was coming with the play ideas, the challenges of dialysis became much easier to bear. In a peculiar way, I actually looked forward to the dialysis treatment. After completing "Get Out of the Box", the nice guy, who was formerly a wild and abusive man, came to mind. I pictured him as an egotistical woman-abusing thug and created a character named, "Rip." His character represented one of the most stereotypical types of men in the inner city.

It was exciting to think how neat it would be to write a play that showed "Rip's" offensive attitude toward his girlfriend, whom he regularly cheated on. The audience would experience the ugliness of such a widespread personality type and feel empathy for those whom he kept under his control. Then a moment of salvation would happen to free the girlfriend from "Rip's" emotionally draining clutches. Once again, I had time while on dialysis to write. So I wrote "Rip" and other characters with him in a short play called, "I Believe." Again, Denise joined with me and composed the music.

When I completed "I Believe" the beautiful lady in her late sixties who did not want to go to the nursing home came to mind. I wrote a short comedy play about a nursing home called "Home Sweet Home." With the AIDS patient in mind, I wrote a short play with a stereotypical black Baptist preacher. With traits familiar to several patients, I wrote a short play called, "Help Me", that included salvation of the "Rip" character from "I Believe." Up to that point, I had never been a writer, but it was like something had been turned on in my head, that I couldn't and didn't want to turn off. I looked at this as a new gift from God for both Denise and I because the creativity for each of these plays superseded my prior knowledge.

It was nearing the spring of 1999; kidney stones were still a prevalent nemesis making life challenging. My doctor told me that surgery to remove my kidneys would be my only option to completely stop the kidney stones from developing. I did not have enough kidney function to preserve life outside of dialysis, but the little function I had did bring some benefit. There were obvious pitfalls associated with no kidney function while on hemodialysis. Removing both kidneys was a last resort treatment and a dangerous procedure.

I lived in a bittersweet world of trauma from disease and creative sparks of drama. Denise and I started getting a drama team of friends together to learn and perform the musical theater we had written. I longed to be off the dialysis machine to personally perform in the plays.

Do Not Pass Me By

In April of 1999, a few weeks after starting drama practice, I received an unexpected call from the transplant group of Vanderbilt. They had a potential kidney for me! As I hung up the phone, I didn't know how to feel. I was so shocked I could hardly believe it. Was I to just stop everything and take this risk or just pretend it never happened? When I thought about it, my stomach got tight, as I was so nervous. As I continued to think about this possibility, I also felt like this could change my whole world and I could have more flexibility in life's daily activities. This would mean *freedom,* and I could live a normal life again. *A normal life?* My emotions were flooding my brain with thoughts.

> *I can live like other dads and play ball with my son without nearly passing out. I can have the energy to do the theatrical plays given to me without looking and feeling so sickly. Could this be God's plan?*

The kidney was coming from a 19-year-old male donor who had lost his life in a car accident. A dialysis patient in Memphis had rights to the kidney first. At any rate, according to Vanderbilt's protocol, the kidney was going to be transplanted in someone within hours. Though remote, the potential for a new kidney came with a bombshell question, "Should I agree to be second in line for this kidney?"

There were major transplant drawbacks for me. First, the doctors had repeatedly cautioned me that my type of kidney disease could quickly destroy a transplanted kidney as it did my original kidneys. I found myself in a huge test of faith in which I could be in great peril whether or not I received the kidney. This devastated me, leaving me thinking, *What the heck? I can't win either way.* Second, kidney transplants required many strong medications with numerous side effects, which also included the strong possibility of becoming sterile. Third was the statistical proof that close relative kidney donors had a much greater success rate. Finally, the kidney matching process included good, average, and poor donor matches. Kidney transplants had a low degree of success rate if the kidney was a poor donor match. The nineteen year old's kidney, doctors stressed, was a poor match.

On the bright side, I remembered that only a properly working kidney could produce enough urine to stop the painful kidney stones and prevent dangerous surgical kidney removal. I did not know which way to turn; accept the kidney that may not come to me anyway or reject it and be doomed to the risks of kidney removal surgery. *Which should I choose, Jesus?*

Two very important people helped me make a decision to accept the potential kidney. My five-year-old son, Chazn, was the first. I remembered several months earlier, when I was highly disappointed in the risks of getting a transplant and thus couldn't see a valid reason to ever have one. I was sitting on the couch at home, as Chazn sat on the couch beside me and asked, "What's wrong daddy? Why do you look so sad?" I told him, "Daddy wants to get a new kidney like you have inside of you, right there in your side, but a new kidney won't work in me." Chazn then said, "Jesus can heal you and you can get a new kidney."

I looked at my innocent little boy, who had no possible medical knowledge, and said, "Son, you don't understand. No kidney will work in daddy." He repeated himself as if I never said a word, "Jesus can heal you and you can get a new kidney." His mother and I had taught him about Jesus and here he was innocently reminding me of God's promises and love. The faith of this boy was too great to overlook.

God, are you speaking to me through this little child? Could this be true?

Denise was the other influence in my decision. She didn't say much about it. If I agreed to the potential transplant, she was going to stand with me. With a sigh, I said, "Let's try it." I went to Vanderbilt to be prepped for surgery in case the man in Memphis did not take the kidney. While laying in the hospital bed waiting, the surgeon informed me that the man in Memphis wanted the kidney. An ambulance was taking the kidney from Nashville to Memphis as we spoke.

Bye bye kidney. This feels strange, God. I just know You wouldn't play a trick like this on me. What are You doing?

I had built up the strength to face major surgery that could prove useless or even more damaging to my body. My hopes were deflated even though I didn't expect the man to turn down the kidney anyway. I called Denise and informed her. Then I put on my clothes and began walking out of the prepping room, but just before I reached the door, the surgeon came quickly walking from the telephone. He said that the Memphis man was too sick and weak to go through the transplant surgery. The odds were in my favor! The ambulance had turned around and was heading back to Nashville with a kidney for me! A waterfall of emotion poured all over me. I felt as though I was on a roller coaster, but found myself at the top ready to take the ride of my life!

> *God, you won't leave me during surgery will*
> *you? I know You won't, because you are my*
> *true Father.*

I practically lost my breath as I was hit with the reality that the transplant surgery and its risks were happening that night. I called Denise and she had someone bring her to the hospital for support. A few hours later, around midnight, the medical staff took me into surgery as I waved to Denise. After being put to sleep, I awakened to the sight of Denise and many tubes in my body. My first thought was: *Did it work?* Anticipating my concern, she encouraged me with a smile by saying, "The kidney is working." The moment the surgeons connected the new kidney it began producing urine immediately. I sighed feeling great relief as if another set of prison doors had been opened before me to set me on a path to freedom. This time however, I was unashamed and ready to tell about what I had suffered and how God brought me through it. The doctors said they had never witnessed such a quick response as in my case. It fascinated them as they witnessed a miracle! I thought to myself,

> *"It's true...my son was right! Jesus DID take*
> *the disease away!"*

The possibility of transplant rejection from the kidney

disease was still at hand. A day later the doctors brought me astounding news. There was no sign of the FSGS disease that destroyed my original kidneys! The disease was gone and the kidney was working properly against all odds. I was now free from a life on a machine!

One of the first reality checks to a transplant patient is the fact that you now have a VITAL organ in your body that previously belonged to someone else. It's a fact of medical science that a person's immunity system, as if being invaded, will tend to fight against a new organ and try to stop its function. To stop this from happening, doctors prescribed medications that lowered my immunity system, and thereby making it easier to contract even simple illnesses that could prove life threatening for me. With all this in mind, I had a choice to make, either I stay secluded from people as a result of this transplant or get out and be free to grow more in service to others.

Love Was The Answer

The prescriptions resulted in me having to take 50 pills a day! I took about half in the morning and half at night. There were prescription drugs specific to help lower my immunity system, drugs to lower my blood pressure, drugs to lower my cholesterol, drugs to fight against side effects of the other drugs I was taking...drugs...and more drugs! When I was just starting as a rookie in taking the medications, I drank so much water to swallow the pills that I could hardly move. Eventually, I would learn to swallow several at a time; totally disgusting, yet entertaining to family and friends that were brave enough to watch. I was so grateful that God provided a way to save me from the pains and weaknesses associated with dialysis. I didn't complain.

A lowered immunity system makes a transplant patient more susceptible to sickness including the many that are passed along by children. To add to this challenge, if a transplant patient contracts a sickness (including the common cold), it tends to take a higher toll on the body's system and can sometimes cause hospitalization due to progression of the sickness. Transplant doctors strongly advise new transplant patients to wear masks around people, and to stay far away from groups of children. My transplant protocol was to stay away from any crowd for six weeks and to wear a disposable mask in public settings. Did I take this important advice?

This protocol was a difficult one to imagine following, as Denise and I still were worship leaders for the children's choir at a large church. Interacting with people, including children was our way of life! The children were eagerly awaiting my return. Being in the presence of dozens of children singing with germs flying throughout the room was out of the question even with a disposable mask according to doctors.

Also, another important consideration in this protocol was the surgical site of where the transplant surgery took place. I needed to be careful in the types of movement I made. Too much movement could cause a dangerous rupture.

Surely, the Lord had not shown me this ministry calling, only to have me neglect it...

In spite of all this, I believed that God wanted me to get back to the children in the choir as soon as possible, so I totally ignored the six-week transplant protocol. After only three weeks of recovering, without a mask I slowly walked into the church rehearsal room filled with children surprised to see me. I had to frequently keep my own two children from jumping on me, let alone a room full of children excited to see me. Denise and a few of the parents kept the kids from stampeding me, but I could not resist hugging the children. I cried softly as I felt their sincere joy to see me. *Oh, how I missed this!* One by one little arms wrapped around me and my heart was flowing with joy, unspeakable joy from such a welcome.

Denise and I believed the transplant was a gift allowing us to show more of the love of Christ. We knew without any doubt God had given me that kidney. Why would He give me a new kidney and take away my calling? In fact, He wasn't taking anything away at all. Why would He separate me from the children that needed my support in various ways? He was giving so much, more than we could see or realize at first. Freedom came when we 'by faith' completely disregarded what the doctors advised...to obey the One Who heals and provides health. Oh, by the way...PRAISE GOD! I never caught a sickness while in ministry with a group of children.

3-2-1...ACTION!!

Within a year, Denise and I had formed a musical theater group called A.C.T.I.O.N.: an acronym for Anointed Christian Theater Inspiring Our Nations. In April 2000, at the Tennessee Performing Arts Center (TPAC), we performed the short plays that I wrote while on the dialysis machine. Nashville residents also heard me performing the monologue of, "The Sunday Morning Christian" on a popular radio station leading up to the performance.

Nashville's *Tennessean* covered the event by writing an article with a heading that showed how my kidney transplant inspired the play. That was not altogether the case. The inspiration came from witnessing testimonies of patients who, like me, experienced the love of God in some of the most hopeless situations.

Chapter 11

"UNITY" IN THE HOOD

Drama Production Leaders

After the Tennessee Performing Arts (TPAC) production in 2000, the pastor of our church was not only pleased with Denise and I working with the children, he was also impressed with our musical theater talent. As a result of the positive outcome at TPAC, our pastor increased our position to serve in dual roles of leadership in drama ministry and children's choir worship. We welcomed the opportunity to sharpen our musical theater skills within the church. Denise and I also received great favor from the church staff and members.

Our lives were rapidly changing. Never before had Denise and I been given this amount of responsibility and leadership status. I was exceedingly thankful to God for healing me of the traumatic kidney disease, and I felt alive again. We were growing in ministry and considered our family complete with two wonderful children. And yet although it had lessened a short time after my release from prison, the fear of others discovering my past still haunted me.

A Miracle of Love

In the early summer of 2000, Denise came to me again with one of those small rectangular devices with the cylindrical hole. I knew the purpose of the device, but not why

Denise was bringing one to show me. The doctors had made it clear that I would most likely be sterile due to the many transplant medications. Evidently, Denise and God did not listen to the doctors. As it turns out, Denise was pregnant with our third child. We joyfully laughed at our new gift from God. Wow! What a shock! I looked into Denise's eyes and she was happy. We thought of another little pair of pattering feet running through our house. You can imagine us laughing inside:

> *They said it wouldn't happen again. Boy, were they wrong! Will this one be a boy or girl?*

Our position included writing and producing two full musical theater productions, one in the fall and another in the spring. On occasion, we performed skits for the congregation at the Sunday morning worship service. Visitors from other churches throughout the city would attend our productions. It gave me much fulfillment and pleasure knowing that God was using what He gave us to bring encouragement to others.

A few weeks before the fall 2000 performance, we were scheduled for a routine ultrasound at Vanderbilt Hospital. To our dismay, there was a serious problem detected so we were immediately scheduled for a follow up ultrasound with a specialist a few days later to confirm the matter. We were so nervous, though Denise had suspected something all along and wasn't as shocked.

The doctor came and told us that our baby did not have a properly formed esophagus. This was an extremely life threatening birth disorder called congenital esophageal atresia (EA), which represents a failure of the esophagus to develop as a continuous passage. Instead, it ends as a blind pouch. But that wasn't all, we were also informed that there was a possibility of a defective trachea as well that would definitely cause death at birth. We were given the option to have an abortion as soon as possible to avoid the stress of wondering if the baby would survive at birth.

We immediately, without wavering, said, "No, we will not take that option." The doctor gave us a strange look as though she thought we were trying to be brave. We told her that we would choose to believe "our God" for the health of the baby and expressed to her our faith in Him healing the condition. We truly believed he would not die, however, deep inside we were so afraid of what we would face upon his birth. We wondered if we would have to care for him in special ways.

With all that we had been through over the past few years, we walked out of the hospital dazed, walking away in one of those moments of silence, when there's not much to say. Agonizing thoughts plagued me as I wondered,

> *Is this all my fault? Did this happen because of all the drugs I take? Oh No! How can I live with that guilt? God, I am trusting in you and not what the doctors are saying. I can believe for our son.*

After going back and forth in my mind, I decided to believe for the best. We began to encourage one another hoping faith would get stronger, so I spoke with certainty that God was going to take care of everything. Denise agreed.

As we got closer to home, the fear we felt leaving the hospital left us. We knew that this new baby was a gift from God, and Denise and I had not forgotten how Jesus had given me the gift of life and healed me from the kidney disease. We had not forgotten how He continually kept me free from sickness in the midst of kids unknowingly passing germs. We had not forgotten the many blessings that we had received from God's love. We refused to believe that our son would be born unhealthy. After revisiting all the times God had come through for us, our faith shot to the roof! We were affirmed knowing He would prove only His love and faithfulness to us once again.

Prayer for a Miracle!

We prayed for our son almost every day. Denise reminded God of all His promises of healing and stood firm believing for a miracle. In spite of what was going on around us, we pressed on with the fall drama production rehearsals and performance. As a result, the drama production turned out to be a great success. We did not let the ultrasound diagnosis hinder our ministry focus.

At the turn of the year, 2001, each ultrasound showed our child still having EA. Towards the end of the pregnancy one of Vanderbilt's most reputable physicians explained the many conditions of the birth disorder. We went through the normal scheduled counseling appointments that would prepare us for what seemed inevitable and necessary actions after delivery. We appreciated her kindness and empathy, but I think she thought we were slow of understanding, because we would never accept that he would be born unhealthy. One night, Denise went to a prayer service to receive healing prayer for our son from a visiting pastor from Indiana. She left that service feeling assured and confirmed of God's intervention.

A couple of weeks prior to our child's birth, we went for another ultrasound. The same reputable doctor brought a small group of medical students to show them what congenital esophageal atresia looks like on an ultrasound. To the doctor's amazement, she could not find the birth disorder on the screen. Our child had formed a perfectly healthy esophagus. Totally healed! It was priceless seeing the look on the doctor's face! We unashamedly gave thanks and praise to

God. Soon thereafter Denise gave birth to our third child, a son. We named him Jordan, which means, "cause to descend or flow down". When Denise was given this name, she believed that would happen to the enemy who was after his health. We knew that God would cause the enemy to "descend or flow back down" to where he belongs and we would be victorious in the battle. This experience gave us an amazing faith that would take us to yet another level with God. We were strengthened in the fact that absolutely nothing could prevail against us because GOD was on our side!

As months passed, Denise and I developed strong relationships with church leaders and parents of the children's choir and increased in knowledge in the area of musical theater. In July of 2002, we were asked to perform a drama ministry seminar at a national convention of a large church denomination. We spent an evening at the convention teaching on various aspects of drama ministry, and we were received in high honor. We were facing an opportunity to travel or do workshops at conferences for this denomination, with the possibility of promotion and a raise in this. Things started to look very promising.

A Change is Coming

At the end of 2003, Denise and I sensed a change coming to our lives. Studying the Bible had become one my favorite things to do far above watching television. I would get up early in the morning before my kids and begin studying. After my two oldest kids were off to school, I would study more. After studying the entire Bible, I would study it again. It felt as though God was unlocking hidden messages before my eyes! I noticed that God's primary desire was for mankind to love one another. This included loving the least fortunate.

We enjoyed our positions in drama ministry and choir, but we strongly felt like God was calling us to serve another group of people. We just didn't know where or how. Our financial situation was taking a turn for the worst. It was a disaster! Our rent was raised a couple of times, food costs were higher with our growing family, and we kept missing payments on our vehicle while dishing out money to mechanics to keep it running. Our finances were falling apart. Then one day something happened that transformed me beyond no return. I totally and completely surrendered to Jesus in a way I had never done before, giving all of my fears and heart to Him. I was filled tremendously with His precious Spirit and I haven't been the same since. A new kind of warrior was introduced to me...Holy Spirit! Everything changed.

I had become closer to God, but unfortunately, we still didn't have enough money to pay our bills even after adding the drama ministry and choir income to my little Social Security Disability check. Quickly things started to fall apart. First, our car was repossessed. Then we were threatened with eviction from our apartment due to late payment fees. We could not explain why God would want us to resign our ministry positions within the church, while simultaneously battling to maintain housing. Nevertheless, after consulting with our pastor, we did the unexplainable and said a loving "good bye." I recall us asking: *What next God?*

Denise and I desired to attend another fellowship and learn more about them, because we knew God was sending us. Within a couple of weeks our car problem was solved. Upon hearing of our dire situation, a nice couple there was moved with compassion and gave us their old 1988 Fleetwood Cadillac. This was the largest and longest car I had ever driven. My small body nearly disappeared in it. In my experience, the only place old long white Cadillac's were ever seen was in the rough inner city low-income areas nicknamed, "The Hood." I was just waiting for the police to pull me over assuming I was a drug dealer, a pimp, or a preacher. But that gratefully never happened, and we were tremendously thankful for the gift. This was a new concept for us...we had never witnessed such a giving response to our need and thought it to be kind of strange for people to love and care for us without "knowing" us.

In the meanwhile, teaching principles of the Bible had become a heavy desire of mine. As I spoke with people at church and in every day life, I was compelled to share Scripture on virtually any topics of discussion in a spirit of love. It was life changing to see how a simple truth from the Bible could heal the most difficult situations. God began sending several people to me and the need for encouragement grew and grew. Eventually, God placed within my heart to combine some of those needing encouragement into a weekly Bible study group. It was amazing how strong His presence began to flood our small home.

ONE DROP OF HIS LOVE

One day I was lying in my bed and something incredible happened to me that transformed my life yet again to draw me closer to God. I will share from my journal:

> *In what appeared to be a dream, I awoke and was led by the Holy Spirit to look up to heaven. I saw a door high in the sky open to a glorious kingdom with golden light. Jesus looked down at me from this spectacular place of Holiness and one tear of love dropped from His eye and fell on me. The warmth of His love enveloped my whole being. All I could see was a magnificent blue mist surrounding me that carried the revelation of His love. There are no words on earth to describe the feeling of exposure to the pure love of God.*

Suddenly I realized that this mist was also His breath. I begged and begged and begged. Then I begged some more for Him to not release me from this place of utopia in the breath of God. Then He made me realize why the experience came in the form of a tear. He was longing more than I for the time when we will soon join together in eternity away from the physical world in a paradise whose atmosphere is designed only with the breath of His love. He was longing more than I, for me to realize that I could receive awesome degrees of His love from glory to glory even now and share it with others!

What a refreshing encounter with my eternal Father in heaven! I noticed a different feeling inside unlike any other in my life. I felt like a true warrior that possessed the one weapon that could defeat anything: love. I finally came into a fresh revelation of my desire to be a Samurai warrior when I was a little boy. The secret weapon in the heart I had always wondered about; it was LOVE! I was destined to experience a life with no father, so I could someday identify with those to whom the Lord would soon send me to serve. As the Lord sent adults or children to me for encouragement or advice, I looked at them differently, more warmly, more sincerely, more...fatherly. I no longer looked through the lens of my eyes to see, because I had begun to look through His eyes. One drop of His love is ALL it took. I was forever changed!

Moving to "The Hood"

In the winter of 2004, one of my Bible study students was a young lady who had a one-year-old child. She was a Tennessee State University graduate and worked for a non-profit organization that aided low-income entrepreneurs in starting their own business. She lived with her child in a rebuilt income based inner city community, commonly known as "subsidized housing," better known as the "Projects." We told her how close we were to eviction. She suggested that we move to the community where she resided.

Never in our life had Denise and I considered moving to the projects. This was far from any financial solution we had discussed. Denise's immediate response was "No, absolutely not. That is not an option for us. I've heard too many bad stories about the hood. We have children. Thank you for your advice and idea, but no thanks." And my initial thought was *Whaaa...?* Unanswered questions and concerns filled my mind.

> *What would people think of us, not to mention Denise's family? How safe would it be for our kids? What kind of schools did they have in the inner city by the projects? What would we be doing in "The Hood?"*

For ten years, we had never been threatened with eviction; then we received a notice from the apartment manager. This letter shocked me so much. I stood frozen as I looked at it. *What!? God what are you doing?!!* Regardless of how things were looking, we had so much faith that God would supply for us once again as He did countless times before. There was absolutely no doubting He would do it once again. *After all these years are you moving us out?!!!* I will never forget that day, throwing that letter down in dismay. Sometimes He supplies in ways you least expect, leaving you standing with your mouth hung wide opened in awe. The truth is, we had no choice. God obviously had a different plan than ours about moving. It didn't take long for us to realize this plan. We did what we always tended to do. We trusted and obeyed.

Almost immediately, my Bible study student took us to meet the manager of the "project" housing. The waiting list for residency was long and the prospect for a vacant home was not yet available. It would be months or possibly years before we would be accepted as residents. My student friend pleaded with the manager explaining our urgency and the fact that I was on disability with a wife and three children. She convinced the manager to allow us to move to the top of the list. Our application was accepted and after being displaced for two weeks and living with friends, we happily moved our family into the inner city. Although monthly rent fluctuated from our initial rent of $70 per month, it remained extremely manageable.

A Candy-Coated Invitation

The first day after we moved in, a little girl knocked on our door. I asked her what she wanted, and she never spoke. The more I asked, the more she just stood there smiling. I called Denise to the door and told her. Denise went to get some candy for the little girl. Strangely, the little girl went home next door to us without ever speaking.

The next day, several new kids came to our door including the non-speaking little girl. They all wanted candy, and Denise gladly shared. The other children told us that the non-speaking little girl was deaf and mute. Suddenly it all made sense. Our hearts were opened wider as we looked upon this child with great compassion. As the days passed, more and more kids came for candy. We found out that there were over fifty kids on our street. One piece of candy to a deaf little girl caused our house to be visited regularly by children throughout the neighborhood.

Parents, who were mostly single mothers, saw and heard from their children how nice we were treating them. The parents would then stop by and ask us to watch their kids after school until they returned from the store or work. We would have children dropped off at our house from parents we hadn't even met. At times, we didn't have much to give while barely feeding ourselves, but somehow God would provide us with snacks to keep the kids happy. Love always provides for the need. We always had "enough."

In the spring of 2005, we had become somewhat enthusiastic seeing kids flock to our home each day. Our three children also welcomed all the new little friends. Our kids soon became the well-liked kids in the neighborhood. One morning lying in bed while the house was quiet, Denise pulled out another small rectangular device with the cylindrical hole in it. This time, my eyes really popped wide open...another baby?! I guess God thought that three children in a 3-bedroom subsidized housing unit and a house full of neighborhood kids were not enough. All I could say again was, "Wow!"

When public school let out for summer break, the management of "project" housing thought we had set up an unauthorized daycare service. We were frequently threatened with a fine because the many kids were destroying the grass that the management had planted in our yard. The only thing that could help the situation was to keep the kids out of our yard space. *How could we do that to them?* After all, they had contributed to beautifying the landscape around our unit by helping Denise and a dear friend plant flowers. Children don't care about rules and regulations. They only care about giving and receiving love. At the risk of being evicted, we refused to stop the neighborhood kids from coming to our home.

Little Frightened Eyes

During the following school year we witnessed a tragedy that inner city kids often suffer. My little girl, Caylin, was in the first grade at the time. I would regularly walk her to and from school with her best friend. The little girl lived with her auntie, and each day her dad would come to walk her home from school. We were so pleased to see and know that she had a father that would invest time in her, because this was an extremely rare sight in the hood.

One evening Caylin and I took a different route home from her friend and dad, because they decided they would go to the corner store. Late that evening, we got a call from Caylin's friend. Her daddy had been killed in front of her on their walk home. This event naturally traumatized the little girl and devastated us. Can you imagine? It was a wake-up call that caused us to see the plight of the children. We allowed the little girl to spend the night at our home several times to love on her and nurture her emotional well-being. We were once again moved with compassion as she shared with us all that she was facing. The only weapon we had to fight despair within that child was love. It was something money couldn't purchase and something that was free to give. One of our friends from church brought us a large teddy bear for the child, which we gave to her as a gift of love. The next time we saw her, the little girl told us that the teddy bear made her feel like she wasn't alone.

Forever Papa Joe

For months we had gotten to know children and their families throughout our inner city community. We consoled and prayed for people in the community with various traumatic situations in their lives. We started to see God heal them and free them from frightening situations. Amazing! Soon, however, we learned of practical needs of families when our daughter came from her friend's house and told me, "I turned the faucet on but no water came out." Her friend's family of six had no running water, because they had no money to pay the bill. Often times for the families, it was a choice between enough food for the week or maintaining utilities.

As we heard stories of various living conditions, we

took the need beyond "us" by going to others at our loving church. As the plight of the community was brought before them, donations were given to help provide a little relief. We found that the same kind of love we received when we had need was now shown for the people in our community. We had discovered most of the homes were single mothers or single grandmothers who "lacked" enough support. Some had financial assistance from the government for food (food stamps), yet in most cases the allotted amount would be insufficient for a month's grocery bill. We too were in this system of poverty, experiencing it ourselves, thus the burden grew to help others. This was the beginning of inner city ministry outside our home.

In January, our fourth child was born. We named him Elijah, which means, "My God is the Lord." The name, Elijah, remained in my heart for the inner city kids because of God's Word concerning the children and fathers in Malachi 4:5-6, which states: *"Behold, I will send you Elijah the prophet ... And he will turn the hearts of the fathers to the children, and the hearts of the children to their fathers..."*

Within a month after Elijah's birth, Denise and I were asked to train a choir of kids from a different inner-city community across town to sing at the National Day of Prayer ceremony to be held at the Ryman Auditorium. It was during one of those rehearsals, that I experienced the "Will you be my daddy?" event that I shared in the introduction of this writing.

Denise and I were never the same. We realized that it was God's providence to move us into the "projects" where so many underprivileged and at-risk children were crying out silently for help and love. We accepted the call to be surrogate parents to an unknown number of oppressed children, and the mission to unite others for the same cause. After that name-changing event with the children asking for a daddy, I became forever...Papa Joe.

Elijah's Heart and "UNITY" Are Born

We trained the choir and they sang at the famous Ryman Auditorium. When we returned home, we were compelled by God to GATHER THE CHILDREN! We knew beyond a doubt that the time had arrived to initiate a choir of inner city at-risk children. We were to use what God had given us to touch their hearts with the love of Christ. We named the choir, "UNITY" to represent the thousands of children crying out in need throughout the city of Nashville and throughout the nation.

I believe this choir of inner city children was the foundation for everything that was to come. The praise of these children did something in the kingdom of heaven that only children could do. It was undeniable that Christ loved this choir:

"But when the chief priests and scribes saw the wonderful things that He did, and the children crying out in the temple and saying, "Hosanna to the Son of David!" they were indignant and said to Him, "Do You hear what these are saying?"

And Jesus said to them, "Yes. Have you never read, 'Out of the mouth of babes and nursing infants You have perfected praise'? (Matthew 21:15-16)

During this process, God brought a few others along our path who had different backgrounds, but the same heart for these children. We had finally come to the point where we stopped looking at what we *didn't* have and started looking at what we *did* have in our hands to give and answer His call. We didn't have to look far. What would once start out as a Bible Study group, turned into a remarkable leadership team! We were not aware of all the gifts and talents He had placed in our ministry team, but we were to soon find out! You see, we learned along the way that God knows EVERYTHING and we don't. It is wise to only do what He says and not what we think. We would combine our money together to buy inexpensive food for the kids to have lunch.

Oh, how exhilarating it was to watch as God highlighted individual gifts of the team that had become like family. He had placed in our midst all we needed to accomplish His purposes. Each one had a passion from the Lord that translated well into what we were doing. Some helped teach songs, some prepared food for the kids, some organized paperwork, some took pictures and videos, some kept order, and some watched the younger siblings of the choir kids and so on. Along the way we had learned a very important fact about walking in faith: If God tells you to do something, He will provide the means to get it done. It doesn't matter what it looks, feels, or seems like, He will honor your obedience and make provision for His purposes. This whole process of events was utterly amazing and a MIGHTY faith builder!

To position our ministry team for growth and the ability to receive surplus from people and organizations all over the country and abroad, we applied to become a 501(c)3 nonprofit organization. Within a few short months we were established to take tax-free donations. Taking into account the Scripture that inspired the name of our son, Elijah, we wanted a name that would join the hearts of surrogate parents with oppressed children. We named our organization, Elijah's Heart. Enthusiasm grew in our ministry team, as we were quickly moving forward. The ministry team consisted of ordinary people with hearts to serve and love. That's IT! We didn't profess to *know* anything, so He gave us wisdom and we obeyed Him. That's ALL!

We treasured our small ministry team that was united with us to bring children out of their at-risk environments to help teach them discipline, unity, and love with music and song. We felt this was a depiction of how the Church can function outside the walls of the building. Jesus made a profound statement, "Those who are well have no need of a physician, but those who are sick." (Mark 2:17) By learning of His ministry from the Gospels, we saw that He was in the midst of the broken hearted, impoverished, depressed, outcasts, and poor! As we obeyed what He told us to do, we were able to sit back and enjoy watching Him do His God thing.

In our obedience to God, we first sought out children in our own community to become part of "UNITY." The Lord conveyed to us that we were to gather children throughout Nashville. However, due to the lack of transportation we decided to start reaching those around us. We would take the city one street at a time, starting with our own! Then take the community! Initially, we had over thirty children join.

Several months after the choir was established, a member at the church we attended informed us that he owned a bus sales company. He offered to let us use very attractive new buses to transport the kids to rehearsal locations, stating that he had always felt that God wanted to use Him in this way. We were overjoyed. With this blessing, we quickly expanded outside of our neighborhood and sought out children in housing "projects" throughout Nashville. We took choir interest fliers and spoke with dozens of families. As a result of this effort, "UNITY" grew to over 80 children.

Our move to "The Hood" was becoming unlike anything we had ever imagined. The sounds that came from the voices of the children in "UNITY" stirred the souls of people at every engagement, because their lives were being stirred by love from our ministry team. "UNITY" beckoned people to give support to the poor and the underprivileged in various ways.

Chapter 12

PAPA JOE'S WALK OF LOVE

It was becoming apparent to Denise and I that "UNITY" was not a final chapter in our ministry to inner-city children. "UNITY" was an igniting point, a banner that was raised to bring awareness of their existence! Living within a poor inner city community and being so closely involved in the lives of these children, we saw needs unknown to the general public. Those that live outside of the poor inner city housing districts often had no understanding of the difficulties and struggles within.

Eyewitness To Need

At the afternoon choir rehearsals, Denise and I learned that in order for the children to focus on singing, lunch had to be served prior to singing, because many of them appeared to have not eaten all day. Our ministry team's hearts were grieved watching little children gobble down three hot dogs as if someone was going to take them away. As Denise and I led the kids in songs expressing God's love, I witnessed them enjoy singing praises. We had rescued them momentarily from conditions of abandonment, poverty, distress, and for some abuse, and brought them into an environment with a ministry team that cared for their physical, emotional, and spiritual needs by giving love and attention and yet, we would shortly thereafter bus them back home into their environment. This broke my heart each time.

I could feel the heaviness weighing my heart down. I couldn't keep a dry eye when I thought of the gravity of this situation. I felt so helpless once again. Someone had to do something! I later learned this was the "burden" given to me by God.

One evening after dinner with our family of six, I was cleaning uneaten food off our kid's plates. I threw away three biscuits and of course, green vegetables. I had a dream later that night. In the dream...

> *I was throwing in the garbage can the same three biscuits uneaten from that night's dinner. I looked up and saw a little dirty girl about seven years of age on the other side of the trashcan. She held out her hand as a sign of asking for the three biscuits. She looked desperately hungry. Suddenly, many hungry dirty little children appeared beside and behind her. There were children from all races throughout the world and they all were motioning for the biscuits. I wondered why they were all there asking me. What could I do? Then out of the blue, the face of the first little girl changed to the face of my daughter, Caylin. An urge of desperation came over me to get the biscuit to the little girl, who now was my child. Then suddenly the faces of all the hungry dirty little children changed to only the faces of my children. I was urgently trying to see how I could get the biscuits to the children, who now were my children from all those races.*

I awoke from the dream sweating with eagerness to

provide hunger relief for every hungry child. The dream seemed so real. It was so vivid. I had taken this issue so lightly, in a sense not giving it much thought at all. You don't think of these things until it hits your own life, then you wake up to the reality. Never again, would I neglect the needs of less fortunate children. I believe Jesus knew that the dream would ignite a fire in my heart to rescue all ages and races of children from the predicament of dire need.

I would never have a heart of apathy as I did when I watched television documentaries of starving kids in Africa and the Middle East, and extremely hungry ones in America, who needed supplemental food to stay healthy or to focus on education. A burning desire filled my heart to search God for ways to help the helpless children.

Help for the Helpless

The vast majority of the children in the "project" communities had parents who received food stamps. As we talked with parents in the communities, we learned the challenges they faced in completing the application process to receive food stamps. Many high school and junior high school dropouts end up in "project" communities. As a result, we met parents who had difficulty simply filling out the food stamp application. We also met elderly people raising their grandchildren in the projects. A family of five siblings, that lived in the projects and were members of "UNITY", were being raised by their sick illiterate grandmother, who was over 70 years of age. She represented numerous households needing aid just to apply for food stamps.

Regardless of perceived qualifications, food stamps are not received and children therefore not fed unless the complete application process is approved. This posed challenges for many unfortunate parents. Often a parent couldn't afford the city bus ticket to get to the food stamp office. Even when a parent managed to get to the food stamp office, it would be a wasted trip without the birth certificates, social security cards, children's shot records, and all the required proof for the food stamp application. Some of these items, like birth certificates, had costs, in addition their distributing state agencies had to be located by directionally challenged parents without vehicles.

Due to the size of our family and low income, we qualified to receive food stamps. Denise and I were not "dead beat parents" as many parents on food stamps are unfortunately stereotyped. On the contrary, after trying to survive on a small disability check, this was a great blessing to us. Out of my own family's need, I had to find the answers to all the food stamp questions and get all the validating paperwork, cards, and certificates to properly apply. It also gave me the opportunity to find the most efficient methods to complete the food stamp process.

A second grade girl in "UNITY" was being raised by her grandmother in one of the roughest "projects" in Nashville. The little girl's mother was in prison on drug charges. The grandmother moved from her two-bedroom home to the "projects" just to be able to afford raising the child. As I visited the grandmother, she asked if I knew anything about applying for food stamps. I was disgusted at the fact that she and this child living in great poverty had gone without meals because of the inability to complete the application process. *Why don't people who could help know all this?* The ability for parents and guardians to get free food for their hungry children was often out of reach right here in America.

As you may have noticed, I'm referring to parents and guardians who honestly would appreciate help in the application process. Of course, those abusing the food stamp system don't realize that they often cause problems for these honest parents. There are plenty of stories of "food stamp kingpins", who lure drug addicted or bill crunched parents to sell the use of their food stamp cards for a much lower cash value. I pray that society does not allow helpless children to suffer for the crime and mistakes of ignorant adults.

I also discovered the common misconception of many in the general public is that enough food stamps are approved and given to provide for a family for the entire month. A common need, even for those receiving food stamps, was simply to have enough food in the house to make it to the end of the month. Food stamps in a very poor household typically ran out at some point within the third week of each month. Since some grocers charge tax on coupon usage with food stamps, saving that way is an unattainable option for some. In our neighborhood, I noticed that the number of children asking me for snacks would tend to increase toward the last ten days of the month.

God's Biblical Word Arrested My Heart

One evening I sat down and again read many scriptures in the Bible on love and helping the fatherless and the poor. Conviction to take action grew deeper in my heart. Messages from God's Word started filling my mind. I remembered:

> *"My little children, let us not love in word*
> *or in tongue, but in deed and in truth."*
> *(1 John 3:18)*

I learned that God created love to be an action word. I realized that the desire to help others in need was placed in my heart by God. But I desired to help many more people than what was available to me. We didn't have the money to assist the way I would have liked to; we too were considered "poor" living in the projects. We could relate to the families, because it was a stretch for my own family to live on our income and food stamps!

Then I read another important scripture from the Bible:

*What does it profit, my brethren, if someone
says he has faith but does not have works?
Can faith save him? If a brother or sister
is naked and destitute of daily food, and
one of you says to them, "Depart in peace,
be warmed and filled," but you do not give
them the things which are needed for the
body, what does it profit? Thus also faith
by itself, if it does not have works, is dead.
(James 2:14-17)*

To act on the Biblical Word of God telling us to help
children and parents in need would take faith far beyond our
income, but faith would mean nothing if we did not do the
work required to help the people. Without faith it was going
to be impossible to please God (Hebrews 11:6). We had to
take the faith steps, even though we DID NOT see where the
money or supply was going to come from.

It was resolved in my mind that if Jesus was compelling
us to feed seven neighborhood children in our little home
each day, then He could give us the supply to feed seventy.
If He could give us the supply to feed seventy, then He could
give us the supply to feed 700, then He could give us the
supply to feed poor children and families all over the city,
nation, and even the world.

Then I read the heart of God the Father for those in the
body of Christ to simply share out of their abundance:

"For if there is first a willing mind, *it is* accepted according
to what one has, *and* not according to what he does not have.
For *I do* not mean that others should be eased and you bur-
dened; but by an equality, *that* now at this time your abundance *may supply* their lack, that their abundance also may
supply your lack—that there may be equality. As it is written,
"He who *gathered* much had nothing left over, and he who
gathered little had no lack."(2nd Corinthians 8:12-15 NKJV)

155

"Abundance" means surplus over necessity. I first thought about the necessity in my own family. Even with our low income, after planning for every meal of the month, we would somehow still have enough to share with others. After research, I learned that there was enough abundance in America to feed other nations. Anyone with a heart to give can give what they have to give. People, businesses, churches, and all types of organizations often had surplus.

All that I read from God's Word implanted a revelation in my mind that energized our ability to aid any number of children placed in our heart by Jesus. The problem with the many children not getting enough food was not a lack of supply, but simply a lack of faith and love in action!

I fell on my knees and began to ask God for forgiveness for all the times of doubting His ability to use us as instruments to feed or clothe the poor, at-risk, and underprivileged children He loved. Although the means were not in the physical, I was left without excuse. Denise would remind me how it never takes a dime from your pocket to do what God tells you to do. It is His pocket and He will make the provision when there's a heart that will obey.

The Walk of Love is formed

Through faith in Christ we found the needed food for everyone who requested it. The whole process of the inner-city mission's tour evolved into the name, "Papa Joe's Walk of Love." Our desire was to visit inner-city neighborhoods throughout the city of Nashville on a rescue mission searching for children and parents who needed help with food and other necessities.

Since 2006, the Walk of Love has impacted thousands of children in eight inner-city neighborhoods throughout Nashville. During this time, God supplied us with tens of thousands of dollars worth of food, clothing, toiletries and other necessities through donations from churches, organizations, individuals and the many volunteers. Communities have come to look forward to seeing the people in the golden yellow t-shirts storm through the neighborhood on a giving spree.

During one of our Walk of Love events, the test of faith was very present. It was Friday, the day before the Walk of Love. We were set to pick up an order from a reputable organization that had committed to supplying boxes of food for over 500 people, mostly children. The volunteers were set to meet us in the morning. The community families had been called and promised that HELP was on the way.

Then we received an unexpected call less than twenty-four hours from the Walk of Love informing us that the food shipment was aborted due to company issues. Just like that... we had NO IDEA how food would get to our families. Our entire ministry team wondered what to do. I felt that calling off the Walk of Love would affect so many and cause many to lose trust in us and judge us as they had other organizations (who failed at helping) by saying, "you aren't really trying to help us" or "you guys are playing a prank on us." I did not want them to view us as "not serious" about our desire to help them. I did not want that at all.

We had no CLUE what God had up His sleeve! We felt so confident that the Lord wanted us to give food to the people, but there was very little time left to do anything. So we waited on Him to give the next order, besides it was His plan and not ours. We prayed. Denise and I had learned so many times in our lives that faith often is not proven unless tested.

About an hour after we began to pray on that Friday evening, I got a call from a lady who had great interest in helping the children through our ministry. She was totally unaware of what was taking place in our dilemma. She called to say that somehow she found $8000 in her bank account that she was previously unaware of. She felt she was to give it to us for the Walk of Love. I shouted to the team what she said. Our praise to God hit the roof. We then knew God had given another way of support that would bless her as well as increase our faith in His divine provision.

Knowing we did not have time to buy $8000 worth of food, we had to receive wisdom quickly. I had the thought of walking by the cash register at the store and noticing the grocery gift cards. That was it! We visited the neighborhood grocery stores and purchased grocery gift cards. We didn't stop there. We located coupons and the best sales. With this information and the grocery gift cards, the parents could buy enough food to stretch to the end of the month.

"God Has Given"

In Spring 2007, Denise came to me again with... you guessed it, another small rectangular device with the cylindrical hole in it. Not planning, we were pregnant with child number five! This time we simply said, "Thank you Lord."

In November, Denise gave birth to our son, Johnathan. His name is consistent with the ministry of the Walk of Love. It means "God has given."

Chapter 13

TEACH A CHILD TO FISH

It is my hope that you understand that Denise and I are examples of how God orders the lives of His children in ways that we would never choose, unless we know the final outcome.

Desire to Break the Cycle!

As you just experienced in the origin of Papa Joe's Walk of Love, our next desire was adequate provision for the least fortunate children in our city, country, and beyond. There is an adage that begins with, "Give a child a fish and you feed him for a day…" There are millions of children throughout the world who are desperate to see more people like the golden yellow t-shirt crew bringing needed food and supplies to their city, community, or village.

The next part of the adage is, "…Teach a child to fish and you feed him for a lifetime." As Denise and I learned more and more about the practical issues plaguing at-risk children, one factor stood out at the top of the list: education. The thing that first caught my attention on the education issue was a situation that occurred with my oldest son's three bicycles when we lived in "The Hood."

I was under the assumption that we could chain his first bike to an immovable concrete handle on our back porch and no one would try to break the new reinforced bike chain that

I purchased. I was mistaken! Then Chazn thought he could ride his second bike down the street to a friend's house, step inside and say hello for a few minutes, and no one would have time to take his bike. That was the day he got better acquainted with the hills of the community while walking home with no bike!

Finally, we figured that the teenage boys from some other neighborhood, who played basketball for a few days in our driveway with Chazn, would never take his third bike off the front porch when Chazn came in to eat lunch. One of the teenage boys was spotted in another neighborhood several times with his friends in the middle of the day on Chazn's bike.

It's this third bike theft that brought an unsettling thought. The teenage boys were being spotted during public school hours. They were all dropouts. I paid money that we hardly had for that bike. I could have easily called the police and confiscated the bike, but my heart became saddened for the plight of the teenage boys. Mercy won out, and I did not call the police. I prayed that the boys' lives would turn around for the good. The burden to break this inevitable cycle of high school dropouts setting themselves up for big trouble assaulted my heart.

Inner-city Schools

Somewhere our system of education failed these kids and thousands like them in America. Dealing with the challenges of inner-city public schools was like walking through a maze. This was foreign to me, because I had changed my attitude in High School for the better. As a fifth grade student, our son, Chazn, attended a local inner-city magnet school with twenty-nine other students in his class. Most of the students lived in poor neighborhoods with no dads. Thirty percent of his class was from other nations and most of them barely spoke English. A considerably large amount of time was spent calming the class down and keeping order. The teacher himself told me that only three kids in the class knew their basic multiplication tables.

These issues and more caused much of my son's instruction or class (lesson) to be in the form of homework. In other words, teachers sent lessons home for "parents" to teach, because they unfortunately couldn't that day due to poor classroom management. I was a member of the Parent-Teacher Association and noticed that this was the case for many teachers. Although this appalled Denise and me, it was not a big challenge for us, but our hearts were broken for the community children. Many of their parents were either uneducated or under educated, and thereby unable to adequately help their children. Homework required the ability to read well. Without the ability to read well, little would be learned. Math homework required knowing basic skills like addition, subtraction, multiplying and dividing.

Another issue was research. The teachers' ambitions were to keep the students abreast of the latest findings in the sciences. Unfortunately, our closest library was four miles away, out of walking distance for the many kids in the neighborhood who had parents without vehicles. I felt like I was back in the days when the computer was new technology, knowing that our family was among the few inner-city parents who owned a personal computer to help their children's study. Parents would ask us to tutor their child who couldn't get the aid they needed at home. It was fun watching Chazn show another child how to maneuver around the computer, but I was disgusted at the fact that the unfortunate child did not have daily easy access to a computer.

If you live in the middle of a trashy society for children like Denise and I experienced, you can't help but be repelled by the bad odor of and the sight of more trash piling up. This is how I felt, unable to make a difference living in the middle of the trashy educational system. The trash I'm speaking of was the following vicious cycle going on with poor inner-city kids. They would start off excited about going to kindergarten. As they went through elementary school, variables beyond the kids' control would cause many to start lagging behind in reading and math, like issues of over-sized and/or chaotic classrooms, little basic reading and math support from poorly educated parents, intangibles like food for snacks or dinner, being surrounded by violence in the neighborhood.

When the inner-city children reached middle or junior high school, I noticed many of them were about two years behind the federal reading standard; sixth graders reading at fourth grade levels, seventh graders reading at fifth grade levels, and so forth. The sexual hormones of the kids would start kicking in, adding a whole new element of distraction. Homework in our neighborhood with some kids often took second place to the battle over which girl was going to win my oldest son.

Many of the high school boys seemed to be sleepwalking in broad daylight. The misdirected young men had reached a state of idleness; walking by our house in sagging pants hanging their heads mumbling to each other. Already far behind in their classes, school had become a burdensome chore. It was "cool" to skip class in groups like the bike thieves had possibly begun before dropping out. The horrifying question was, "How many inner-city youths starting high school actually finish?"

Drugs in the schools were as common as lunch. Chazn had been tempted with drugs among other things from young dealers in the fifth grade. Many high school students were dealing drugs as a career, never planning to graduate and get an honest job. I worked with the apartment association president consoling single mothers who were frightened of high school dropouts who had been robbing homes in the neighborhood.

Home Becomes School

Since Denise and I were at home during the weekday, we began homeschooling Chazn for the remainder of his sixth grade year. Denise visited Caylin at lunchtime a few times during the first few months of her third grade year and was appalled at the daily lunch conversations that took place. She was heartbroken at the fact that the children were discussing topics that could get them into serious consequences once they arrived at puberty. But even more disappointing was the point that children didn't stop their conversations in Denise's presence as though she was expected to join in along with them and take pleasure discussing their sexual awareness and social life. We are talking about THIRD grade!

Although we had planned to homeschool Caylin the following year, we decided to transfer her sooner to a homeschool academy. Thankfully, homeschooling proved beneficial for us in learning and building our children's character. Without the public school experience, we would not have known what was happening in the lives of our dear beloved community children. Our hearts were aching at the potential breakdown that was taking place in schools, the place they should be learning, growing and preparing for their futures. This is why I believe they are "at-risk." It's not just their environment at home, on the streets or in school. It's everywhere.

As I witnessed the inner-city dropout rate, memories of criminals in prison flooded my mind. You can do the research. I was there. The jails and prisons have a disproportionate percentage of dropouts. It all started to make sense to me! Remember, I personally helped over thirty get their GED while I was incarcerated. By the way, I noticed the food stamp office was packed with former high school dropouts. Many were young ladies who gave birth as teenagers and didn't have a recovery plan for school.

Our Walk of Love program revealed to our ministry team

an important statistic. A substantial amount of our city's public school children lived in housing "projects." There were over a dozen communities like ours run by one state agency alone, plus several other privately owned communities scattered across the city. One community alone had over 700 homes usually with multiple children in each home. I was overwhelmed with the thought that thousands upon thousands of children were fighting against a hidden dead end cycle in education.

An Insult to Injury

The missing key of our ministry was support in the area of education. I now had an additional desire to be part of change for these children. In the winter of 2007, I had gotten a lead to a personal grant at a state vocational grant agency. The grant allowed people receiving federal disability payments from Social Security to apply for free funds to start a small business. I thought this was maybe the answer to begin helping the inner-city kids in education. We could help at least thirty students at a time in a school semester. As a result, I placed a learning center within my business plan. We had to start somewhere. Sometimes in the past taking bold steps had caused me to step in dog poopie, but this grant seemed worth a try, besides what did I have to lose?

I spent months writing and modifying the business plan. Some of our ministry team members went with me to speak with the directors of a subsidized housing agency seeking rooms to rent for the learning center. We researched and visited successful learning centers and tested their learning center software. Much to our amazement, the grant agency told me that I was applying for a matching grant. Cash would be matched on monetary or furniture donations. We put the word out on what we needed and were donated a large amount of equipment for the entire learning center. We received tables, chairs, printers, large copy machines, office supplies, and old but workable computers. Denise and I thought, "How good can it get?"

The pursuit of getting a learning center established for a relatively few kids put us on a path of life with a twist no one could have seen coming! When the summer of 2007 arrived, we were actively involved with our various ministries, and as I stated before, Denise was at that time pregnant with our fifth child, Johnathan.

Then came the breaking news, as a resident of subsidized housing on income based rent, I understood that I had to report all income. The Social Security Department under the federal policy of the grant was not considering the donated equipment as an asset. To our seeming detriment my subsidized housing landlords considered otherwise. We had thousands of dollars of office equipment and supplies stored. The total value was being placed in the equation to determine our income-based rent. This meant we no longer qualified to live in the "income-based" housing, our home, anymore!

Denise and I could hardly grasp the unfavorable housing predicament in which we had fallen. What irony. Our attempt to start a learning center in one of the poor inner-city communities totally backfired on us. We sincerely did not know where to move our family, until the young ministry team member, who originally convinced our subsidized housing manager to let us move in years earlier, allowed us to move into her new two bedroom condominium. We were so grateful, yet cried as we packed our bags to leave the community we initially did not want to live. Our hearts were torn and crushed as we looked into the eyes of the community children and even our oldest biological children and told them we were moving. We could see and feel the anxiety in them, but we felt it was something we had to do to help them in the long run. Leaving was a lot harder than we had ever imagined.

The Room of Purpose

About a week later, my pregnant wife and our four children moved some of our clothes upstairs in the little purple room of our friend's daughter. Denise and I slept in the bedroom, and our kids slept on the floor in the small living room downstairs. It was during those times we became increasingly heartbroken for those who were homeless. While still leading volunteers on Walk of Love mission tours throughout the city helping hundreds of inner-city children with food and school uniforms, we secretly did not have our own home. Can you imagine how insane this looked to our biological families? It was admittedly ludicrous! Yet, our hearts were filled with great courage knowing that there was a purpose in it all that led to helping and promoting educational benefits for the children. Oh, and by the way...the meaning of the little girl's name whose room had become our temporary little home was "purpose." We were living in the room of "purpose." It was so humbling, and we will forever cherish that priceless time of our lives.

Just before Christmas, the grant that seemed a cinch that we had modified for months; the grant that caused us to receive thousands of dollars of equipment for a learning center; the grant that gave hope for financial stability; the grant that got us kicked out of our "project" home, was NOT approved! This news proverbially added insult to injury. I left the grant office drenching myself in tears. Not only had I hoped to help the inner-city kids in education, the learning center would have provided income for us to eventually get a house for the first time in our entire marriage.

What a disaster! I came home and fell on the couch, sobbing from feeling so helpless. It was like I was pushing a large mountain that was not budging. I felt like no one cared about those forgotten children. It took me a couple of days to calm down. I battled against stress for a while never thinking we would have been forced to leave the "projects" of all places. It took encouragement from Denise to fight against the horrendous guilt in losing our apartment and leaving the community children we loved so much. At the time it felt like I had even let my own biological children down, trying to help others. We were homeless, and it seemed to be for nothing now! Finally, I came to my senses. We had trusted God for our welfare for many years. It was not time to stop. We found rest in the thought that our situation was far too abnormal to *not* be in the plan of God some kind of bizarre way. We focused on the meaning of the little girl's room in which we lived, "purpose." This also kept us encouraged.

Our friend who took us in got married in the fall of the year. Her husband moved in adding another body to the house. Amusingly, they got pregnant within a week of the wedding, and had a baby nine months later, and we still lived there. Then in Summer 2008, a city codes inspector heard from one of our friend's neighbors that there were too many residents in her condo. I met him outside before he knocked on the door. My family had days to move out or the sheriff's department would be there. We moved our large family to a hotel room for a few days. Although we moved back in as "visiting guests", we knew our time was soon to be expired living with them.

All Our Goods

Before we moved from "the hood" we thoroughly went through everything we owned and assessed whether or not it was of value to us. Then, we place our valuable things in a storage unit, because there was no space of course where we were going to live. We helped our homeowner friend with utilities and eventually the rent also, because she was laid off when her employer closed the company. As our finances became a strain, I could no longer make payments on the storage unit. We were asked to remit payment at a point when we had no money.

To make a long story short, we lost EVERYTHING in the storage unit. We lost all of our furniture, children's favorite items; keep sakes, sentimental items cherished from our own childhood (including the first pair of Samurai Joe's nunchaku) and baby and family pictures collected up until that point. We didn't get a chance to retrieve any of our belongings. It all happened so fast.

Just when we thought we had nothing, we were shown what "having nothing" was really like. It was like our house had burned down suddenly! Denise was devastated over the pictures! *At this point things could only get better, right?* This was the perspective we were forced to see. We had no clue of what God had planned all along.

A Big Surprise!

One Sunday morning, I was the guest speaker at our church of over 700 members. I spoke about the lessons we learned in the lives of at-risk children. My message was a wake up call to the church and a call to action to move out in the love of Jesus to the least of God's children. After the message, a lady came up to me wanting to talk later about our ministry. I learned that the lady and her husband had recently moved to town. For weeks the friendly couple began giving their time and support to aid the children who served in the inner-city choir and the Walk of Love.

Our time living with our friend had come to an end, as we strongly felt directed by God to move back into a hotel for an extended stay to not put our ministry team member's condo in jeopardy. After the friendly couple learned of our living situation and the history behind it, the result was beyond many people's comprehension. The couple felt compelled by God to give us one of the most extraordinary material gifts possible. At the end of October 2008, they bought us a beautiful 4,000 square foot house in Brentwood, Tennessee, just a few miles from Nashville. No rent...no mortgage...no fear of eviction...ALL FREE! Look how GREAT our God IS to us!!!!

Two other awesome families bought all the furniture! It's difficult to express how elated we were at this. The home was perfect for the ministry, friends, children and most of all OUR FAMILY! Upon entering our new home, the first thing we observed was the wall full of recent PICTURES of our children...it was overwhelming that such a warm thought and effort went into this idea. In that moment, we felt God was restoring everything we lost, plus a whole lot more! A home is too often taken for granted in our country. The house included a large open space in the kitchen and living room area. It also included a large bonus room that we made into a television room and meeting room holding at times over twenty-five guests comfortably.

For a full year someone even paid for our utility bills. What a fresh breath of air this season was for us. And that's not all, within a few weeks, another little precious elderly grandmother of a team member drove her van all the way from deep south Georgia to give it to us, because she no longer had use for it. We now had a wonderful new home, paid bills AND a van freely given! I thought of God's purposes in all of what we had gone through...being taken from nothing to standing in a house to which we own the key, plus a key to a new vehicle...WOW! Oh, to understand the plans of a loving Father. My heart is overwhelmed with emotion. For a month every morning waking up seemed like a dream as we basked in the Lord "giving" to us in abundance.

What extravagant Love! Thank you Jesus!
You have given me more than I ever expected
or even deserved.

We continued to home school all our children with aid from teachers in our ministry team. Three months later, the following February 2009, Denise brought to me another small rectangular device with the cylindrical hole in it. Yes, we were pregnant with our sixth child! She was born on October 8, 2009. We named her Shadai meaning God is MORE than enough!

Hope for the Children

Throughout the year of 2009, we kept growing in ministry helping all the inner-city children we possibly could. Our home was their home. It was a joy to see our house frequently flooded with kids. Despite the failure to get the grant, my burden for education advances kept me seeking God for answers. The thought of "computers" in the homes of inner-city children constantly stayed on my mind.

We are all living in the information age. I have watched my own kids become computer literate in a computer-run world. We start our kids learning on the computer before age two. The term "at-risk" when applied to education refers to kids that live in a community or society that lacks the resources to meet children's basic educational needs, such as a safe environment free from violence, a classroom with order as opposed to horse-playing, enhanced training outside the classroom, and proper teaching tools such as up to date books. The deficiency in which inner-city children existed without computers was astounding.

Some states like Tennessee were giving inner-city parents the option of home-based public schools (kindergarten through 12) that came under the title online learning/virtual schools. As I researched and talked with parents I learned that this type of school had been successful for many families. Parents whose children were threatened with bodily harm could avoid violence in dangerous school districts. The students were assigned a teacher, books were used, time on the computer was not extreme, and social activities were included. All books were free. All records and communication were done through the computer. Of course, the limiting factor for most poor inner-city parents was the lack of a computer. Home-based public school was a wonderful discovery, since the hope for a learning center for our community children seemed far, far away from reality.

> *Why can't I just leave this idea alone? Why can't I just face and accept it is not meant to be?*

These thoughts along with others were always present in my mind and still are as I write this.

My Burden!

Amazingly, Denise reminded me while writing this book that I was once a little boy who felt educationally challenged. This explained my burden to not give up on the hope and vision of a virtual learning center, where inner-city homes would possess computers with reading and math software, internet connections to educational sites, and volunteers tutoring the children and encouraging parents. That would start a revolution of success in the schools of Tennessee and ultimately the nation! And she was so right! I was very well acquainted with the condition of an at-risk child. I had to reflect back and marvel over the revelation of my childhood!

Oh, how I was once in their place. I knew the emotional and mental pains of feeling left behind or slow at learning. I knew about peer pressure when it came to not being able to read well. I knew what it was like being that frightened little boy who already felt like an outcast among those who were different. I knew how it felt to be ridiculed and laughed at, because I had a slow start in the system. I knew of the incomplete feeling inside that stemmed from not having a father's affirmation. I knew the anger and discouragement that sat deeply within my heart and mind, driving me to fits of rage. Could that have been one of the catalysts that pro-pelled me into violence?

I wanted to be a hero; someone who would protect those who were hurt by circumstances that were beyond their con-trol. I wanted to help, but something inside me then wanted to counteract unworthiness. I was weak in those years, because I had no self-value. I would beat up bullies trying to protect those who were hurt, but was I really trying to protect myself? How many kids are feeling this same way today? How many of them are looking for a hero? How many of them are in search for someone who will love them? How many of them are waiting for someone to reach out to them? How many of them hope that SOMEBODY will hear their silent cry? I could finally see the purpose. I had to go through those painful expe-riences as a child to establish a memory that would stimulate compassion as it relates to the education system of America's impoverished at-risk children. This is a passion that won't fizzle until it is fulfilled, for the sake of the children, for the sake of America's next generation of leaders!

Chapter 14

A CALL TO LOVE

M any seeming roadblocks to our expectations are actually detours used by God to guide us to become greater servants of love to others. In Fall 2009, one such detour happened in my life that would catch practically anyone off guard. I was asked by an executive producer to use my life experience as inspiration for a movie. Up to this point, the gentleman was aware of only our ministry to at-risk children. Without much thought, my initial reaction was, "You might not want to ask me that question, when you find out the things that happened in my past." EVERYONE would know how awful it was for me to go to prison. The gentleman had lovingly given much time and support to the inner-city children we serve and many other organizations. After my response to his question, I felt accountable to briefly explain my response.

As I confessed my past through tears of shame, the thought of "skeletons in my closet" being displayed to the public overcame me; "skeletons" as you have experienced with me in this writing, like fighting in grade school, using computer skills to secretly hack into restricted sites, battling in a notorious prison, and others. I had concealed my tumultuous past in the "closet" of history for so many years. There was no way on earth I would allow myself to be vulnerable to the masses by making my life or my life with Denise an open book.

As usual, something in the Word of God caught my attention. I remembered the example of the "great cloud of witnesses" mentioned in The Book of Hebrews 11:11 – 12:1. Sampson was mentioned among these heroes of God. Because of his lustful desire, Sampson had turned against God by giving the secret of his strength to a seductive female enemy of Israel. He in turn lost his power to protect his people, but he repented and killed more of the enemy at his sacrificial death than when he lived (Judges 16:30.)

Also David, after killing the giant Goliath and later anointed the king of Israel, allowed his weakness to cause him to sin with Bathsheba and murder Uriah, her husband. David repented and though the consequences of his actions were great, later God blessed David and Bathsheba with a son named Solomon, whom God gifted with the greatest wisdom before Christ (2nd Samuel 12:24.)

Then I noticed that none of the sins or wrongdoings were mentioned when the Bible spoke of the great cloud of witnesses; only the things that they did as heroes of God. The truth was reinforced in my mind that God forgives those with a repentant heart that turn from rebellion against Him to obedience, righteousness and love.

I feel far from being a Sampson and even further from the great King David. I don't compare myself to any of those great heroes mentioned in the Bible, but I thought just maybe God was choosing to use my life's path as a modern day sign of the power of His love to transform mistakes, tragedy, poverty, and trauma into a testimony of victory against all odds. Regardless of how unworthy I felt, the sacrifice of my pride would be a weapon of humility to save oppressed children and encourage adults who feel discontented, depressed and useless throughout America and other nations. I humbly agreed to give my story as the inspiration of a movie whose name bears the description of God's love, *Unconditional*.

By the way, within a few weeks to mark the occasion,

Denise performed her traditional ritual that she had done many times before. She brought to me one of those small rectangular devices with the cylindrical hole in it. Yes, she was pregnant with our seventh child! And so in July of 2011, Denise gave birth to Kyla Shekinah, which means "Crown of Glory."

Through 2010 and 2011 while still continuing in ministry, I had the incredible privilege of working with some of the most godly and excellent moviemakers. The prominent Hollywood actor that played my part was so talented, I should have maybe taken lessons from him on being Papa Joe. I must say that being the inspiration of a movie to bless an untold number of children and families has been most surreal.

Actors and crew on the production set would frequently tell me how the making of *Unconditional* would have a lasting effect on their lives. I'm known to wear one of my "Papa Joe" hats everywhere I go. A white single mother invited to view the shooting of one of the scenes noticed the name on my hat and walked over to hug me. Tears of hope streamed down her face as she expressed the difficult time her preschool son was having coming up without a father.

My most memorable experience of the making of the movie was witnessing the changed heart of a father. An average height muscular African American father living in subsidized housing felt encouraged to confide in me concerning his mistake that previously landed him in jail separating him from his sons. After a brief discussion on God's forgiveness, I witnessed this man forgive himself and watched the love of Christ wash his heart of guilt freeing him to love his children more as a wonderful daddy.

Empowered Men

Please understand, for far too long, I was mad at the world for being fatherless not realizing at the time that Father God was always with me. In college, on the job, in church, and in prison, I've seen too many men like I was, making decisions out of anger. As a testimony, only through Christ can a man truly conquer the troubles of the world with or without a biological dad in the home. The words of Solomon are true: *"He who is slow to anger is better than the mighty, and he who rules his spirit than he who takes a city." (Prov. 16:32)*

I formerly thought that as a man it wasn't "cool" to openly express my emotions and intimate thoughts and feelings to my wife. It had been totally unacceptable to show any hint of meekness or weakness, because I did not understand God's power of grace associated with it. Once I accepted this, I was able to love her in deeper ways. Women need intimate expression from men. They need to feel heard and understood. They need to feel like they are trusted with the dearest thing: your heart. This is how one loves and receives love from them. This is how you truly become "one" with your wife. For the rest of my time on this earth before travelling to my eternal home in heaven, I will "shout from the rooftops" to all men, "The greatest warriors are the warriors of love."

The Role of Godly Women

I fall on my knees to God in His awesome forgiveness, when I think of the audacity of my pride to diminish His gift in my life named Denise Bradford. Because of the love of Christ in her heart, she humbly received me when I considered myself an outcast to all of humanity. She saw something of Jesus hidden in my heart that I had long forgotten. When we were just friends, she proved her faith in God's message in the letter she wrote predicting our unbreakable bond of marriage. She protected my heart from others criticizing my past.

Throughout the entire time of my tormenting life with kidney disease, in my presence she never showed a loss of hope. She never wavered in believing that I would be healed from kidney disease. She never wavered in our son Jordan coming to this earth fully healed. She never wavered when the doctors came to us and told us that Kyla at 19 weeks gestation had not developed her other kidney of all things! She stood firm on her faith in God as Creator once again, and our baby girl is strong with two perfectly normal, healthy kidneys! She has been a testament to me on the healing power of God.

In times of turmoil, I never saw my wife doubt God. She never spoke doubt to me, and she never rejected me. She has been my strength in times I had none. She has been my better half when I fought rejection, disappointment and unworthiness. She has been the definition of love in action. She has helped me become the warrior of love I am today. God's greatest gift to me has been my wife.

Denise initiated our call of ministry to the poor inner city children with a simple act of love. Giving a piece of candy to a deaf little girl. She has been such a powerful example to me. I have watched many oppressed and brokenhearted women transform as the Lord used us to lead them into higher degrees of Christ's love to others. I thankfully acknowledge my wife as an extraordinary woman of God. Next to Christ, my wife is my hero.

Throughout our ministry the role of the godly woman has been spectacular. Women's groups have formed special fundraisers to contribute to the Walk of Love feeding thousands of children. Teams of women joined with us in the 2011 Christmas season to get gifts for several hundred underprivileged children. Pastor's wives have often been the catalyst to unite us in ministry with their church on behalf of Jesus' heart for the less fortunate. There are enormous blessings when men realize the potential of godly women.

Papa Joe – Advocate, Mascot, or Guide

Some people are calling me an advocate for at-risk children. Some people are calling me a mascot, kind of like Ronald McDonald. As a boy, I used to watch old Tarzan movies on television. Sometimes missionaries would come to Africa and need a friendly guide to lead them through the jungle to help those in desperate need. No one knows how the guide learned to speak English, but somehow he must have experienced both ends of the spectrum; he knew those who needed help and those bringing it. I would have loved to be Tarzan, but as Papa Joe, I'm kind of like that guide.

In my heart I feel like the same little child who became Samurai Joe. Although life shaped my heart a bit differently, as a man now, I still have the heart of a protector of the innocent, a defender of love, and an advocate for justice. In my inner most being, I am Papa Joe, made in the image of my Father in heaven. He was and forever will be the Hero I always wanted. I now live for the glory of King Jesus... mighty Warrior of Love.

Wherever the Lord sends us, I pray that Denise and I will continue to be a blessing of support, encouragement and hope helping to lead people through the jungle of poverty, sickness, and oppression.

Your Gift of Love

The most important climax to a book about me really isn't about me at all; it's about YOU. It is a call to love! All the obstacles and victories Denise and I experienced now make perfect sense. God chooses to use ordinary people for extraordinary things. If you feel ordinary, then you qualify! We have learned beyond a shadow of a doubt that a child needs the Father's love and sometimes it takes a few experiences to come to know it. Children love learning of how much they are loved and they learn by observing actions from us. Whether you are a single or married woman you can show the Father's love by sharing it. Whether you are a single or married man, you can show the Father's love by providing it. Whether you are a young child or an elderly adult, you can show the love of God by giving it. Love is a free gift designed to be given freely.

Did you know that you are a gift of love given to this world from God? You have been created to love in your own unique way. Have you discovered it? How can you impact those around you by loving them? In what ways can you give love to YOUR family, neighborhood, city or country? If you look closely, you will see where the need is as it presents itself before you. If you listen carefully, you will hear the cry...the silent cry of those who are discouraged, abandoned, abused and lonely... crying out for what you have to give. Children don't have to be hungry in a country and world of plenty. Our public educational system may be a challenge for many children, but with effort and prayer we WILL make a change. Don't let what you don't have stop you from giving. Only focus on and use what you do have and watch what God will do with your life, regardless of the hardships from your past.

Thank you for sharing this journey with us thus far, and let's continue on! The end of this book is not an ending. It's a beginning!

This is Papa Joe, and from my heart,
I love you!

CPSIA information can be obtained at www.ICGtesting.com
Printed in the USA
LVOW07s0210151114

413712LV00001B/63/P